RACIAL AMBIVALENCE IN DIVERSE COMMUNITIES

RACIAL AMBIVALENCE IN DIVERSE COMMUNITIES

Whiteness and the Power of Color-Blind Ideologies

Meghan A. Burke

LEXINGTON BOOKS
Lanham • Boulder • New York • Toronto • Plymouth, UK

Published by Lexington Books
A wholly owned subsidiary of The Rowman & Littlefield Publishing Group, Inc.
4501 Forbes Boulevard, Suite 200, Lanham, Maryland 20706
www.rowman.com

10 Thornbury Road, Plymouth PL6 7PP, United Kingdom

British Library Cataloguing in Publication Information Available

Library of Congress Cataloging-in-Publication Data

Burke, Meghan A.
   Racial ambivalence in diverse communities : whiteness and the power of
color-blind ideologies / Meghan A. Burke.
       p. cm.
   Includes bibliographical references.
   ISBN 978-0-7391-6667-3 (cloth : alk. paper) — ISBN 978-0-7391-6668-0
(electronic)
   1. Whites—Race identity—United States. 2. Race awareness—United
States. 3. Post-racialism—United States. 4. United States—Race relations.
I. Title.
   E184.A1B8986 2012
   305.800973—dc23

                                                              2012007792

For Ben

CONTENTS

ACKNOWLEDGMENTS

I always try to convince students that shorter papers are more difficult to write than longer ones, and that abstracts are often harder than the paper itself. I had thought that the summary was the hardest thing I wrote for this book, until I got to the acknowledgements. So many people have helped me along the way; I really hope I can at least begin to thank them all.

First thanks belong to my professors in graduate school, especially Dave Embrick; I would be nowhere without his mentoring and support. Dave's insistence on good critical scholarship, his willingness to rapidly socialize me to the profession, and his sense of humor have made all the difference in my career. It was also critical that I learn from the challenges and guidance that my other dissertation committee members, Judy Wittner and Phil Nyden, provided. This team challenged, supported, encouraged, and has continued to guide me in my early career. A brief conversation with Judy at MSS or a quick email exchange with Phil can easily show me fresh wisdom and possibilities, and discussions with Dave always motivate and inspire me. Thank you.

Thanks, too, to my friends and peers at Loyola. I especially want to thank Monica Edwards. Our days in the library as we both worked to finish propelled this project forward in its most trying time, and our friendship before and since means the world to me both intellectually and personally. In the same spirit, I want to thank all of my graduate school friends—your intellect, your ideas, and your friendships sustained me through my deepest frustrations and moments of doubt. Had we not laughed so hard, and talked so deeply, I'm certain I would not have made it.

In addition to this moral and intellectual support at Loyola, I also received institutional support, particularly through the Arthur J. Schmitt Dissertation Fellowship and the U.S. Department of Housing and Urban Development's (HUD) Doctoral Dissertation Research Grant. Both provided valuable resources, both time and financial, to support this research. That support also allowed me to hire a fantastic transcriptionist, Margie Porcella of Chicago Transcription Professionals, whose speed, skill, and conversation also helped tremendously along the way.

I cannot overstate how lucky I feel to have been so warmly welcomed into the faculty at Illinois Wesleyan University. Here I have found a supportive and encouraging home in my academic department with Teddy Amoloza, Rebecca Gearhart, Georganne Rundblad, Jim Sikora, and Chuck Springwood. I have also found friends and mentors throughout the entire faculty and staff at Illinois Wesleyan, all of whom have supported my work and enriched my life. You are truly too many to name, and I hope I've thanked you along the way. I still pinch myself to realize I've landed my dream job with so many fun, hardworking, and inspiring colleagues. I hope to serve with you, "doing well and doing good," for years to come.

I also want to thank our hardworking and engaged students, especially Manish Mandava, who maintained the bibliography for this book. Were I to name the students at IWU, and those I taught as a graduate student at Loyola Chicago, who inspired me, challenged me, and made me laugh on a regular basis, many of whom continue to do so, it would go on for pages. I hope you know who you are, and that you were able to discover my one little lie—you are all in fact "special flowers." I get up in the morning to think and laugh and struggle along with you.

On a more personal level, I must thank The Besties, Mark and Renee, for all their culty camaraderie, and for so regularly "allowing" The Dude to abide. My siblings, Ben and Sarah, are also forever my friends who inspire and challenge me in ways they may not even know. Ben died just before this book went to press, but every word in the previous sentence remains true, so I leave it in his memory and as a way to underline how much I love and respect my sister—I am so grateful for you. My amazing parents, Rod and Theresa, have always been an endless source of moral support, humor, love, and friendship. Thank you for a family full of love and laughter, and for all of your wisdom. And to John-Patrick: your ideas, support, friendship, and love sustained years of work on this project. Thank you.

I would like to extend many warm and repeated thanks to my team at Lexington, especially Jana Hodges-Kluck and Eric Wrona, who helped see this book through the entire production process. I couldn't have hoped for a smoother, more professional, and more enjoyable working relationship. Thanks for all that you do. I also appreciate Laura Reiter's understanding with the delays caused by my brother's death, and for recommending Robert Swanson, who completed the index for this book with speed and skill. Of course, any remaining errors are my own.

Finally, I'd like to thank the people working and living in these Chicago communities who shared their stories, struggles, vision, and time with me. I hope this book is a credit to your hard work, and an inspiration to all those who relentlessly try to make meaning of diversity and social justice.

LIST OF FIGURES AND TABLES

1

LOOKING INSIDE
DIVERSE COMMUNITIES

The face of the United States is changing. As I write this book, the results of the 2010 United States Census are slowly being revealed to the public. With each press release and each round of access to the data, reporters, academics, and other interested parties scramble to make sense of the numbers. We have long known that the United States will not remain a majority white nation. In fact, we continue to learn that we are approaching that change even more quickly than had been initially projected. What will this mean for us as a nation? What will this change look like in our communities? Are we headed for enhanced racial harmony, or a heightening of the tensions historically associated with racial change?

This book provides a glimpse into three adjoining communities in Chicago that have already been living with the kind of diversity that the United States as a nation will soon see. While it cannot predict the future of U.S. race relations, it does offer an analysis of the challenges and opportunities faced by tens of thousands of residents who are already living with the racial diversity that may soon be entering other communities. These communities are far from harmonious; indeed, within there remains visible segregation and a good deal of ambivalence about the role of race and other forms of diversity within the community. At the same time, these are proud communities, filled with many residents, especially their active residents—block club presidents, community organizers, etc.—who are working hard to embrace that diversity and make it last.

This mix of ambivalence and pride is indicative of the broader and at times contradictory aims around diversity in the contemporary United States. In this book I examine how well-meaning residents in these communities make efforts to manage multiple aims. They are working to clean up their parks, support and elevate local businesses, influence their alderman in zoning and development decisions, and make their communities a decent place to live. They also want these communities to be safe and vibrant places to live. As I discuss in chapter 2, much of their community activity is focused around safety initiatives, as they are living in areas that are not just racially but also economically diverse and do carry with them non-negligible crime rates, and development efforts, which range from simple beautification to economic enhancements. They are by and large proud to live in a diverse community; they are well aware that these communities are unique to both the city of Chicago and to the nation as a whole.

At the same time, there is a deep ambivalence about the significance of race, the varying experiences that residents have within a diverse urban community, and which efforts should be undertaken as these communities move into the future. These realities are complicated by the fact that most of the residents actively shaping these communities are homeowners, who have a vested interest in the economic livelihood of the community broadly, and their individual investments in particular. That very fact often puts their individual and economic interests at odds with efforts to sustain the diversity of these communities, as most of the racial diversity comes from the number of rental properties and, in some areas, government subsidized housing. Negotiating these multiple aims is no small challenge. However, examining closely the efforts to do so reveals much about our national thinking about race, the pitfalls of good intentions, and the efforts that can and are being made to support and sustain diversity on the home front.

UNDERSTANDING DIVERSE COMMUNITIES

While most of the United States is still anticipating a changed community as the demographics of the nation shift, some communities, like the ones in this book, are already there. It is not uncommon for communities to have a "moment" of diversity as they transition between white and black, for example, or vice versa. However, it is less common for communities to remain diverse over a long period of time. A number of these communities were identified in 1998 by a team of researchers working together from around the nation, studying these communities in some depth (Nyden et. al. 1998). They found that these communities can be divided into two major categories: communities that were diverse by design and communities that were diverse by circumstance.

To be sure, some of the communities are intentionally diverse, or what Nyden et al (1998) have called "diverse by design." These communities, specifically Milwaukee's Sherman Park, Memphis's Vollintine-Evergreen, Denver's Park Hill, and Philadelphia's West Mount Airy, were hard fought by longtime community members who were dedicated to the principles of not only racial integration but also social justice. Residents of these communities have taken, and continue to take, active and intentional steps to maintain that diversity. In particular, as Nyden et al note, these communities "must make extraordinary efforts to market themselves" (1998, 9). Further, they often make use of community organizations such as churches and block clubs to sustain positive relationships between diverse groups in the community, incorporate the diversity into their decision-making bodies, actively monitor for and work to remedy acts of discrimination, and work to improve the quality of life in the community (1998, 9).

The majority of other stably racially diverse communities, including the ones in this book, are diverse not by intentional design but rather by circumstance. This means that "their diversity is less a product of neighborhood organization intervention and more the product of social and economic forces initially beyond the control of the residents" (Nyden et al 1998, 11). These social and economic forces are usually tied to some sort of change in the community, such as an influx of immigrants, a decline in elderly whites, or some change in property values without the robust market to create full gentrification. These realities of circumstance, however, do not mean that these communities are simply lucky or structured by fate. It still takes community effort and the delicate balance of competing forces to support and sustain that diversity, even by means as simple as promoting their pride in their diverse community.

The 1998 study referenced above was the first collaborative study of the nation's fourteen stably diverse communities, and provided researchers and other interested parties a needed framework, particularly in the distinction between intentionally diverse communities and those that are diverse by circumstance. It examined the internal and external factors that contributed to the creation and maintenance of those communities, and provided what it hoped would be a "tool kit of policies, community-based strategies, and government intervention mechanisms that can work to keep existing diverse neighborhoods stable and be used to develop other diverse neighborhoods" (1998, 6).

It was in a similar spirit that Ingrid Gould Ellen wrote *Sharing America's Neighborhoods: The Prospects for Stable Racial Integration* (2000). In that book she examined the dynamics of the nation's integrated communities and the complex reasons that neighborhoods either embrace or resist integration. In particular, she focuses on the attitudes of white residents and the factors like neighborhood stability and quality of life that impact their willingness to support racial integration (2000, 53). While encouraging for its attention to diverse communities, her analysis does not attend to the complex racial dynamics that I think are necessary to overcome the white resistance she details. However, I agree that diverse communities deserve more governmental support. I borrow on her policy recommendations in the final chapter of this book.

Michael Maly's (2005) book, *Beyond Segregation: Multiracial and Multiethnic Neighborhoods in the United States*, examines the dynamics of unplanned residential integration, the diverse by circumstance communities discussed above. He argues that communities like these consist of numerous subgroups with diverse racial constituencies and also diverse goals, interests, and lifestyles: "These communities differ from well-known models of racial integration . . . in that the established residents and the racially and culturally different incoming groups never intended to be neighbors, and what they have in common is their differences" (2005, 4.). The forces shaping such communities are themselves diverse, and Maly compellingly suggests that "pro-integration efforts could not produce them" (2000, 47). He describes three such neighborhoods in his book, including Uptown in Chicago, and suggests that scholars and community members should develop more complex and less polarized visions of these communities, particularly as they reflect what may well be the nation's future.

In 2006 William Julius Wilson and Richard P. Taub published *There Goes The Neighborhood: Racial, Ethnic, and Class Tensions in Four Chicago Neighborhoods and Their Meaning for America*. In contrast to Maly's book, Wilson's book is a somewhat cynical examination of the forces that prevent integration. In particular, he finds that social organization in the neighborhood is key to neighborhood stability. Without a strong neighborhood base to resist or buffer demographic change, the tendency has been rapid racial turnover and re-segregation. Despite this key insight, Wilson's book analyzes ethnographic research conducted from 1993 to 1996, which makes its publication in 2006 somewhat peculiar. Further, it excludes any current literature on racial attitudes and residential housing choices, in favor of an extended metaphor borrowing on 1970s political science research. As such it delivers little currency descriptively, theoretically, or practically.

In 2006 Camille Zubrinsky Charles published *Won't You Be My Neighbor?: Race, Class, and Residence in Los Angeles*. Charles has written several important articles about racial integration and its link to attitudes and racism, and this book represents the core of her independent research as a doctoral student. She finds that people of all races tend to desire racial integration, while also wanting to preserve a sizable number of same-race neighbors. However, whites are considered the most desirable neighbors, and blacks the least, which impacts residential choices. While her work draws upon an impressive range of literature and presents a large amount of data, the central question is tied to individual housing preferences rather than complex neighborhood dynamics and does not differ significantly from prior studies. Further, this book, like Wilson's, draws upon data that is now outdated, and like Maly's and Ellen's, is primarily demographic and statistical in its analysis.

Finally, the most recent book exploring the dynamics of diverse communities is Elijah Anderson's (2011) *The Cosmopolitan Canopy: Race and Civility in Everyday Life*. For Anderson, canopies are public spaces, such as markets or parks or business districts, where a diverse group of people are able to get along to preserve the public social order. He focuses primarily on behavior in these settings, and the mostly-positive interactions that take place within. He also focuses on "the ways in which the promise of the cosmopolitan canopy is challenged by recurring situational racial discrimination or by the occasional racial incident" (2011, 157) but does not analyze how these expressions coexist. While noting that they do coexist is an important recognition, and while I share his hope that "no forward movement in this long process is possible unless the races share space at close enough range to interact with one another" (2011, 148), the book is relatively surface-level in its analysis. It simply suggests that busy urban locations that are utilized by a racially and ethnically diverse group of people will make people more tolerant of and interested in diversity. As you will see, my book looks much deeper into those dynamics, detailing the pitfalls of the contemporary racial system even among those tolerant toward and supportive of diversity.

While studies like these are a good start, many are still dependent on survey research and demographic analyses, which can only tell us so much. Scholars have noted that we are "near the limit of what can be accomplished through the analysis of publicly available census data" (Logan et al 2002, 320). As Camille Zubrinsky Charles (2003) notes, this type of data can't "account for the manner in which respondents' attitudes influence their residential outcomes" and its "inability to capture the dynamic nature of residential segregation" (p. 199). Maly's study incorporates qualitative data alongside his demographic analysis, but his focus is broad, based around his argument that circumstantial diversity is worthy of further examination. Anderson's is rich descriptively but thin analytically. Further, while I draw upon his findings throughout this book, public spaces are only part of what keeps a neighborhood diverse and socially just.

My focus is tighter in this book, and in many ways deeper. It is tighter in that I am looking only at three adjoining communities in Chicago. While they are stably racially diverse, and diverse by circumstance, my goal is not to push urban sociologists or those studying residential racial segregation to change their theories about urban life. Instead, I provide what may be a deeper look into these communities. I do this by examining the complex thinking and discussion that happens inside of them, especially as it relates to diversity and its associated community efforts. This probes deeper than statistical analyses of attitudinal data have done to date. I also consider how national thinking about diversity

and race impacts that thinking and residents' social action in these communities. I do this because I think this in-depth look reveals a number of
contradictions and pitfalls that stem directly from our national thinking
about race in the contemporary United States. At the same time, I think
that the lessons learned from the desire of active residents to reconcile
these contradictory aims can be useful to the diverse communities that
are likely to follow. I also believe that the commitment and efforts that
the residents in these communities take, despite their pitfalls, are both
inspiring and instructive to others.

AMERICA'S THINKING ABOUT RACE

Communities like the ones in this book are rich places. They allow us
a glimpse into what could be the future of our nation. That future is
one that, for many, is laden with hope and pride. They are also in some
ways a litmus test for United States race relations. Given our racial past,
and our deep uncertainty about how to handle the realities of racism in
the present, they are fertile test grounds to learn what works and what
does not as communities like these increase in number. As Michael
Maly argues, "To understand race relations in urban areas—how race
shapes urban space—diverse . . . communities deserve close attention
as unique and varied urban spaces. They are harbingers of the future of
race relations in cities and the nation" (Maly 2006, 47).

It is difficult to consider the future without taking serious account of
the past. It is no secret that the United States has a difficult and shame-
ful past when it comes to racism and ethnic discrimination. However,
beyond admitting the horrors of slavery and Jim Crow racism, studies
find that most Americans remain unwilling or unable to meaningfully
discuss racism, especially as it continues in the lives of well-meaning
people. This is likely because the national discourse on race, beginning
after the Civil Rights Movement of the 1960s, has been one that has
de-emphasized the significance of race in favor of individual achievement. Nationally we believe we have removed all barriers to achieving
the American Dream. This view is technically accurate: the combined
efforts of the Civil Rights Movement made state-sanctioned segregation and discrimination illegal. In theory, legally, there should be an

equal playing field in the United States, where individual efforts are not stymied by discrimination and opportunities are equally available to all.

The reality, as critical race scholars continually demonstrate, is quite different. While the Civil Rights Movement removed the legal barriers to individual achievement, it did nothing to remedy the generational impact of privileges for whites, especially in housing, education, and wealth. The discourse around race shifted after the Civil Rights Movement as well, claiming that now that opportunities were legally open to all, any individual failings were a result of either individual choices or the influence of "culture." Indeed, the Moynihan Report in the 1960s confirmed what many Americans had suspected even before the legal barriers to equality were removed: that it was not racism but a "culture of poverty" that held racial minorities from achievements. As such, ideological weight has been added to continued systemic disadvantage.

The problem with the "culture of poverty" is that it has always been a theory. It has never had much empirical support. Repeated studies have found no significant difference between racial or cultural groups in terms of their work ethic, motivation, emphasis on education, drug abuse, or other typically associated factors (see Iversen & Farber 1996; Wilson 1997; Compton-Lilly 2003; Lareau & Horvat 1999; Saxe, Kadushin, Tighe, Rindskopf, & Beveridge 2001, to name just a few). Still, a combination of legal victories that theoretically and individually create equal opportunity, the continued belief in equal opportunity as a guiding principle in American life, and the belief in a culture of poverty have created confusion as the United States faces continued differential outcomes by race. It has also fostered a "new" racism.

This racism has been called symbolic racism, modern racism, subtle racism, laissez-faire racism, and most recently color-blind racism. What all findings share, regardless of terminology, is the word racism. This may be confusing to some, given the abstract support of equal opportunity and the disavowal of "traditional," overt racism that the ethic usually contains. Bonilla-Silva (2003) has called this "Racism Without Racists" for this precise reason. As he writes, "this new ideology has become a formidable political tool for the maintenance of the racial order. Much as Jim Crow racism served as the glue for defending a brutal and overt system of racial oppression in the pre-Civil Rights era, color-blind racism serves today as the ideological armor for a covert and institutionalized system in the post-Civil Rights era" (2003, 3). He further argues, "Shielded by color-blindness, whites can express resentment toward minorities; criticize their morality, values, and work ethic; and even claim to be victims of 'reverse racism'" (2003, 4). While this the thinking about race is abstract and neutral, the logic is flawed factually and helps sustain the racial status quo, making it a form of racism. The full impact of color-blind ideologies in these neighborhoods is explored in chapter 3.

It should be noted, however, that despite the emphasis on this "new" form of racism as of late, it should not be assumed that traditional forms of racism have completely disappeared. A recent study (Holthouse 2009) has noted a rise in race-based hate groups since 2008, affirming the suggestion that the election of Barack Obama could invoke racism rather than prove its elimination. Leading anthropologist Jane Hill (2008) has documented the persistence of white racism in the United States in quite overt forms, and Joe Feagin's current work is outlining the perpetuation of a centuries-old white racial frame, which he defines as an "the broad, persisting, and dominant racial frame that has rationalized racial oppression and inequality and thus impacted all U.S. institutions" (Feagin 2010, ix). Tyrone Forman has been tracing a rise in racial apathy, a concept which "captures the ways in which whites many publicly express indifference or lack of care about racial inequality while at the same time continuing to hold anti-minority views" (2004, 51).

It is in the context of this national thinking about race that I study social action in racially diverse communities. As indicated above, a large body of literature documents the prevalence of color-blind ideologies in the United States. What is less obvious is how they relate to specific events, which can be understood as the result of racial projects (Omi & Winant 1994). This book examines how that thinking about race translates into a variety of community efforts. Further, it also demonstrates how national thinking about race is experienced in unique local places. As Jason Rodriquez notes, "Racial ideology is experienced in distinct locations, even as it is shaped by discourses circulating at a national level and spiraling out of a racialized social system. Specifying the distinctly local manifestations of the dominant racial ideology extends our knowledge of how ideology operates in the everyday lives of individuals" (2006, 663). Examining the local manifestations of the dominant racial ideology in a racially diverse community has the potential to test the limits of such an ideology, and examine its fault lines.

This book raises a number of critiques of the thoughts, discussions, and efforts that community members in these communities undertake. However, the goal of this book is not to document missteps in some the few, fragile communities that have been able to maintain their racial diversity. Rather, it is to examine how the well-meaning, pro-diversity, deeply committed members of this community try to make sense of what are in the end conflicting goals: to live in a community where race does not matter, and to sustain the racial diversity that makes their community, and as explored in chapter 5, their choice to live in them, unique. This is the core of the ambivalence and the pride that I detail throughout this book.

THREE CHICAGO COMMUNITIES

This book examines three communities on Chicago's Northeast side: Rogers Park, Edgewater, and Uptown. While they adjoin one another at the far northeastern tip of Chicago along the lakefront, they are in many ways distinct communities. Having a better sense of these communities, their history and their present arrangements, provides important context for the in-depth analysis that will follow in the remaining chapters of this book. As a doctoral student at Loyola University Chicago, these were also communities that I knew and called home for six years, from 2003–2009. I lived in an apartment in Edgewater several blocks south of Loyola in Rogers Park, and the vast majority of my shopping, dining, and time spent in parks and on buses were in all three communities.

Readers unfamiliar with Chicago should first understand that the city is divided into 77 community areas, as seen in figure 1.1. Sociologists established these areas in the 1920s while studying a wide array of topics related to urban life. In fact, the only adjustment to these community areas since that time has been to split Edgewater from Uptown; they otherwise remain unchanged and provide a common cultural basis for residents in the city. Further, Chicago remains a deeply segregated city. A recent report suggests that Chicago ranks fifth among the nation's metropolitan areas in residential segregation, with race rather than

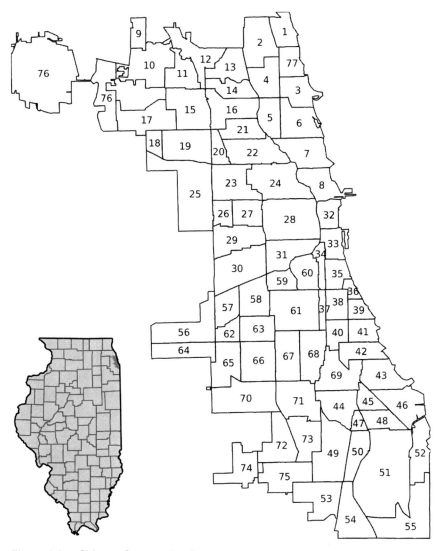

Figure 1.1. Chicago Community Areas

income being the primary factor for its segregation (CURL 2006). Chicago has been home to a long history of violence, restrictive residential covenants (see Schwieterman and Caspall 2006, 28–30 for a cursory but useful overview), and a host of other urban policy decisions that have given the city the racial segregation that remains today.

Despite that reality, pockets of racial integration have been created and maintained. In the following sections I introduce the three adjoining communities whose active residents I interviewed for this project. I briefly explore their history, their community structures, and the political issues that faced the communities at the time I conducted my research, from 2007 to 2009. I also try to provide a sense of their "character" through the voices of participants in this study, to provide a sense of how the communities are understood by their own residents. I supplement this with materials from community organizations and other secondary sources, in order to round out the descriptions. I hope that readers will have a sense of familiarity with these communities as they read the interview excerpts in the remainder of the book.

Rogers Park

Beginning at the north end of the city, the first community in this study is Rogers Park, sitting directly south of Evanston, Illinois. Nine miles north of the Loop, Rogers Park (see figure 1.2) currently has some of the most affordable housing stock in the city, as well as the most direct access to Lake Michigan for its residents, both in small sections of private beach (often available to members of condominiums) and in its public parks. Rogers Park is also home to Loyola University Chicago, and was home to Mundelein College, a private Catholic college for women which was incorporated into Loyola in 1991.

Rogers Park was a distinct village during the 1870s, and annexed into the City of Chicago in 1893. One final annexation in the area north of Howard Street, at the northernmost tip of Rogers Park, in 1915 created the city and community boundaries that remain today. A rail line serviced Rogers Park as early as the 1860s, which helped to foster the creation of very large lots for homes for "vacationing" Chicagoans in that period. The population grew dramatically in the early 1900s, when the Howard Street train line was added and more multiunit rental buildings were created (Mooney-Melvin 2008; Mooney-Melvin 2003; Ebert 2001). That train line remains as part of the current CTA elevated train system.

The housing stock in Rogers Park shifted dramatically, with the rest of the city and much of the nation, in the World War II era. In Rogers Park larger apartment units were divided into even smaller units. Irish and German immigrants had lived in Rogers Park during its early years.

ROGERS PARK

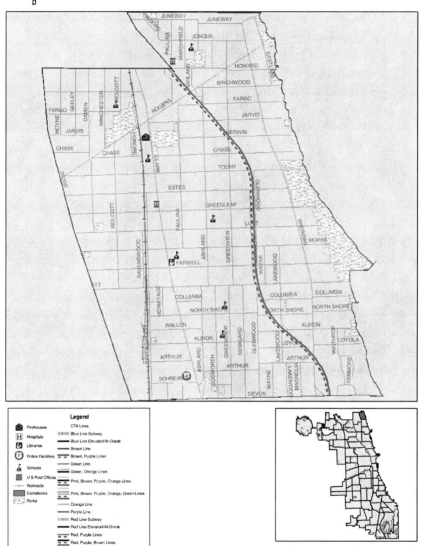

Figure 1.2.   Rogers Park Community Map

Copyright © June 2010, City of Chicago

Once those groups gained access to the suburbs and more desirable areas in the city in the 1960s, they were replaced with Russian and a variety of Eastern European immigrants. The subdivision of units during this era and its increased housing density created more revenue for property owners and also housed a displaced population from urban renewal programs in the 1970s, when blacks, Latinos, and Asians began to settle in the community (Mooney-Melvin 2008). These rental properties quickly deteriorated. As gentrification scholar Neil Smith notes, "Owner occupiers in the housing market are simultaneously both consumers and investors; as investors, their primary return comes as the increment of sale price over purchase price. The landlord, on the other hand, receives his return mainly in the form of house rent, and under certain conditions may have a lesser incentive for carrying out repairs so long as he can still command rent" (1979, 544).

It was in this era that Rogers Park gained the racial diversity it retains today. While, as table 1.1 shows, the numbers have shifted among racial groups by decade, it has retained its racial diversity and is widely regarded as one of the most diverse communities in the city. This is despite a dramatic upswing in condominium conversions since 2000, according to a local community organization who studied the issue in 2006 (Lakeside CDC 2006). Several Rogers Park residents commented that the economic downturn at the end of the decade may have "saved" the neighborhood's diversity despite those condo conversions. That issue gained some national attention on a March 27, 2009, episode of *This American Life*, a popular program on Chicago Public Radio, which featured the efforts of some new condo owners working to stabilize and maintain their own buildings despite failing absentee landlords.

At a glance the racial diversity appears anything but stable, especially when compared to Uptown and Edgewater. As Nyden et al have noted, "Racial change has occurred in Rogers Park. However, 'flight' or

Table 1.1. Rogers Park Racial Diversity 1980–2000

Percent of Total	White	Black	Latino	Asian
1980	70	9	12	7
1990	45	25	20	8
2000	32	30	28	6

Source: US Census

'panic' by white residents is not occurring" (1998, 23). It also holds the distinction of being one of the few communities around the nation that has maintained its racial and ethnic diversity for at least 10 years (ibid). Diversity also remains one of the key distinctive elements of the neighborhood, as the interview excerpts in this book will reveal. Like all three communities in this book, it is diverse by race, ethnicity, sexual identity expression, politics, and income.

The median household income in Rogers Park has remained relatively flat between 1990 and 2000, moving only from $31,646 to $31,767 (Chicago Fact Finder 2009). The housing stock remained relatively stable between those years as well, going from 82.9 percent rental in 1990 to 81.4 percent in 2000 (Chicago Fact Finder 2009). In 2006 the Lakeside Community Development Corporation (Lakeside CDC) conducted a community housing audit in order to determine the impact of recent development on Rogers Park's rental housing stock, which Lakeside CDC links specifically to the maintenance of its racial diversity. This study found that between 2003 and 2006, the rental housing stock had been depleted by 17.4 percent (Lakeside CDC 2006, 3). Further, they found that racial disparities in homeownership rates had widened. While, again, the economic downturn that began in 2008 may have offset this trajectory, the impact of changes in the 2000s remain to be seen.

Rogers Park's community structure is centered around relationships with its alderman, who since 1991 has been Joe Moore. Unlike the community approval process in Edgewater and the umbrella organization network in Uptown that I discuss in later sections of this chapter, Rogers Park has a loose network of organizations such as the Rogers Park Community Council, Lakeside CDC, and "DevCorp," which is a pro-development organization. Rogers Park residents, unlike Edgewater and Uptown residents, were also not active in block clubs at the time of my research. Matthew, a Rogers Park resident, offered the following perspective on its community structure:

I mean, I think in Rogers Park, and specifically in Rogers Park, I think that there is a pro growth cadre of organizations and leaders that are very much working on a growth strategy. That's implicit, based on the type of work that's coming out of some of them. So I would put Dev Corp in that category. I put the alderman's office in that category. I put Loyola University in that category.

And to the extent to which that results in displacement or results in people finding housing more difficult and so on and so forth, it's a concern, but it's not going to stop them from doing what they're doing. They are committed to a particular strategy. And in my mind it's not a particularly public strategy where people are saying our goal is to turn Morse Avenue from small-scale, low density Mom and Pop thrift stores type stuff that poor people can shop at to high-end condos over restaurants, and make it a cultural destination. Well, they don't say it that way, but the reality is that's what they're doing.

That is not to say that Rogers Park residents are not active and organized in efforts to shape their community. Instead, most of the active Rogers Park residents that I met were organized in at-times informal, largely grass-roots forms of organizations that, like Matthew, opposed such a "growth strategy."

Rogers Park also has a very active online blogging community. Several bloggers were very active at the time I conducted this research, and many community residents discussed reading them regularly. In fact, in 2008 Rogers Park was named one of the Top 10 "Bloggiest" neighborhoods in the country (Outside.In 2008). Particularly active and well-known are several conservative and libertarian blogs, which keep tabs on crime, the alderman, state and city spending, and critique what they see to be the shortcomings of liberal and progressive efforts in the neighborhood. While Edgewater and Uptown also have place blogs that serve similar functions, they are either less visible in local politics, as is the case in Edgewater, or more tightly tied to issues of political concern, as is the case in Uptown more broadly.

Edgewater

Directly south of Rogers Park, along the lake, is Edgewater (see figure 1.3), the community where I lived during my six years of graduate school. While it functions as a cohesive whole, Edgewater residents typically separate discussion into its geographical segments: the section nearest the lake where I lived, known as the Winthrop-Kenmore corridor; the section west of Broadway where million dollar single family homes and tree-lined streets once served as a prominent suburb for Chicago's elite; and Andersonville, a commercial and housing district on

EDGEWATER

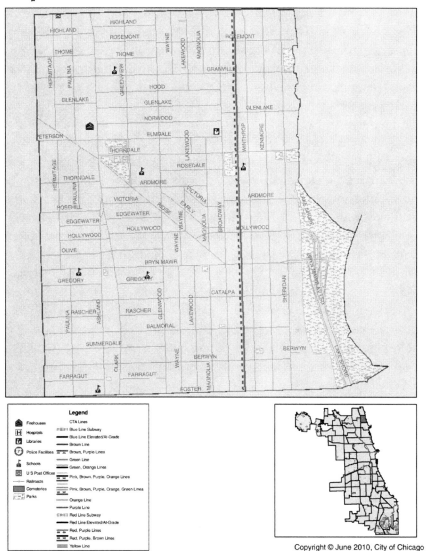

Figure 1.3. Edgewater Community Map

Edgewater's west side which is the historic home to Chicago's Swedish population as well as to much of today's visible gay and lesbian population. Edgewater lies directly between Uptown and Rogers Park, six miles north of the Loop. Lake Shore Drive currently ends in its geographic center, and a portion of Loyola University's Lakeshore campus sits just within its northernmost border. This makes Edgewater a particularly high-traffic area, especially given its many high-rise condos and apartments along the lake.

Edgewater and Uptown share much of their history, as Edgewater was the original name of the development area during the 1800s. Property owners in the 1970s felt that Uptown's reputation for poverty and social service organizations was harming the image of the community and petitioned to create their own distinct community area, a status finally awarded in 1980. Like Rogers Park, this area was not densely populated in the early days of the city. There were isolated celery farms in the area, until a developer created mansion enclaves along the lake for Chicago's wealthy families to use as a second home (Seligman 2008a). Several of those mansions still stand today.

Single family homes were built and today are largely maintained west of Broadway Street in Edgewater, although it is not uncommon to see multiunit condos and three-flat rentals interspersed with these single family homes. Many of the mansions directly along the lake were demolished in the period following World War II, an era in which dozens of high-rise units and other multiunit dwellings were built along Sheridan Road next to the lake (Edgewater Historical Society 1991). The area between the high-rises and Broadway Avenue is referred to as the Winthrop-Kenmore corridor, a strip of housing which became notorious for its often poorly-built and -managed four-story rental units, or "four plus ones," which catered, as in Uptown, to transient renters and the poor. During the 1980s the Winthrop-Kenmore corridor was referred to as "Arson Alley" for the propensity of management companies to torch their buildings for insurance profits. Today the Winthrop-Kenmore corridor is still stigmatized by many of Edgewater's residents for its history, despite the relative safety and continuing development of the neighborhood.

Edgewater is widely regarded as diverse among its residents and by the city at large, and at least through the 2000 Census, it had retained its

Table 1.2. Edgewater Racial Diversity 1980–2000

Percent of Total	White	Black	Latino	Asian
1980	63	11	13	10
1990	51	19	17	12
2000	48	17	20	12

Source: US Census

status as stably diverse. Table 1.2 provides a breakdown of Edgewater's racial demographics in the 1980, 1990, and 2000 census. Edgewater has experienced racial and socioeconomic diversification much more recently than Uptown, with its white population in 1970 at 94 percent (Maly & Leachman 1998, 139), making the 63 percent white population in 1980 a rapid shift. However, this trend closely mirrored the loss of white population in the city as a whole during those years (Maly & Leachman 1998, 139), and as the table indicates, the racial diversity has remained relatively stable since then. Its economic status has also been stable, and remains highest among the three communities examined in this book. In 1990 the median income in Edgewater was $33,010 and in 2000 the median income was $35,987 (Chicago Fact Finder 2009). The percentage of rental housing in Edgewater was 71.6 percent in 1990 and 68.2 percent in 2000 (Chicago Fact Finder 2009).

Development in Edgewater has been tightly monitored by the use of Alderman Mary Ann Smith's community approval process, which I discuss again in chapter 2. This process makes use of the 19 block clubs throughout Edgewater, which are tied in not only to Alderman Smith's community approval process but also to the Edgewater Community Council (ECC), which serves as an umbrella organization for the community's block clubs, businesses, elected officials, and community organizations. Their stated mission is "to serve all the people of Edgewater whom comprise a mosaic of various racial, ethnic and socio-economic groups, multiple faiths and political views. ECC encourages the maximum participation of residents to promote the physical, educational, cultural, recreational, social, charitable and economic development of the community" (ECC 2009). Although Mary Ann Smith's community approval process does create conflict and contention over specific planning and zoning decisions, the dissent is often among individual neighbors rather than among organizations, as has been the case in Uptown.

Unlike Rogers Park, the block clubs in Edgewater are very active and served as the primary site of involvement among the Edgewater residents I interviewed for this book. While the block club structure is not as small as the micro-communities I will discuss in Uptown, there are well-known and often-referenced divisions within Edgewater. Most residents make distinction between the high-rises along the Lakefront and Sheridan Road, the Winthrop-Kenmore Corridor running between the high-rises and Broadway Street, and the area west of Broadway populated by single family homes and desirable brick condo buildings. Some also include Andersonville, a commercial and residential area that is a part of Edgewater despite being widely perceived as a distinct community.

Uptown

Of the three communities in this book, Uptown (figure 1.4) has easily received the most attention from other scholars and those interested in urban life. Uptown has for decades housed the highest proportion of social service agencies in the city, and has a long history of receiving immigrants, the homeless, and the mentally ill. It was a central community in Eric Klinenberg's (2002) *Heat Wave*, an award-winning sociological study into the non-natural causes of death in Chicago's 1995 heat wave. Before that it also served as the site for Todd Gitlin and Nanci Hollander's famous *Uptown: Poor Whites in Chicago* (1970), which explored a group of poor migrant whites from Appalachia who moved into Uptown during the 1960s. The book detailed their radical politics and political organizing against the Chicago machine's welfare system. Uptown was also featured in Michael Maly's (2006) book *Beyond Segregation: Multiracial and Multiethnic Neighborhoods in the United States*. Even today Uptown is well-known among Chicagoans for its contested history and visible poverty. It stands four miles north of the Loop directly adjacent to the lake, and is the southernmost of the three adjoining neighborhoods whose residents I interviewed for this book.

Uptown was not densely populated in Chicago's early history. Home to Swedish and German farmers in its early years, it too was a site for the development of vacation homes and mansions for Chicago's elite during the late 1800s. Later development incorporated more mixed-family dwellings west of what is now Broadway Avenue, as well as a

UPTOWN

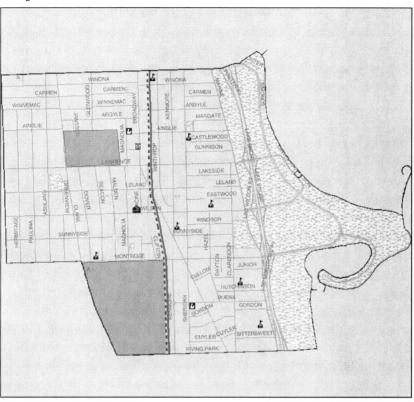

Legend

Firehouses	CTA Lines
Hospitals	Blue Line Subway
Libraries	Blue Line Elevated/At-Grade
Police Facilities	Brown Line
Schools	Brown, Purple Lines
	Green Line
U S Post Offices	Green, Orange Lines
Railroads	Pink, Brown, Purple, Orange Lines
Cemeteries	Pink, Brown, Purple, Orange, Green Lines
Parks	Orange Line
	Purple Line
	Red Line Subway
	Red Line Elevated/At-Grade
	Red, Purple Lines
	Red, Purple, Brown Lines
	Yellow Line

Figure 1.4. Uptown Community Map

train stop along a now-defunct North Shore Line. This train line also facilitated the growth of Uptown as a residential and recreational area. This destination market was bolstered in the early 1900s when the Central Uptown Chicago Association promoted the area as being Chicago's New York City. This is evident in the naming that took place in this area: Uptown became the official community name, Broadway Avenue was created, and various shopping districts, department stores, theaters, and ballrooms were built and frequented by its residents and by visitors to the area's many luxury hotels (Seligman 2008b, Marciniak 1981).

Things began to change in Uptown soon after the Great Depression. In 1933 Lake Shore Drive was extended several miles north, making it easy to bypass the community when traveling between downtown and newer developments to the north. The changed housing market after World War II also prompted a large-scale conversion of the large luxury apartments into smaller units, which were notoriously rented out for profit with minimal oversight of leases and credit terms. As in Rogers Park and Edgewater, these primarily attracted a transient and poor population. This affordable rental housing stock also attracted immigrants and other migrant populations at the time, such as Native Americans, Japanese Americans, and poor whites. The State of Illinois took interest in this area at the same time, steering mental health patients from their closing facilities into Uptown's rental stock (Seligman 2008b).

A number of social service agencies also established themselves in Uptown to serve the poor and immigrant populations who had recently arrived in the area. Uptown continues to receive a large immigrant population from around the world today (see Hanson 1991). Uptown's development in the years after the influx of both the social services and the populations that they serve has been hotly contested, which some argue has been the key element in helping it retain its racially diverse population (Maly 2006, 72). The creation of Truman College, one of Chicago's city (i.e., community) colleges, in 1976 in the heart of Uptown, provoked debate about the services for the poor and their potential displacement. These debates coalesced around two prominent organizations—the Uptown Chicago Commission (UCC), which organized in 1955, and the Organization of the Northeast (ONE) in the 1970s, both of which remain intact today (Maly 2006; Marciniak 1981; see Bennett 1993).

The UCC's stated mission is "to improve the quality of life for all Uptown residents." Its primary areas of focus are public safety, community development, and zoning and land use (UCC 2009). UCC is generally pro-development, as characterized by Maly: "UCC members and supporters accuse the many social service providers of not helping the poor get out of poverty, but rather of maintaining a dependent and needy population to serve. . . . Instead, promotion of neighborhood upgrading is necessary to prevent it from becoming a slum and to maintain integration" (2006, 71). UCC members or affiliates whom I spoke with for this book generally reflected that perception. In particular, the vast majority of residents on this "side" of the development debate strongly opposed Alderman Helen Shiller, who they argue retained a "poor vote" in order to continue to ensure her seat in the city council. Anthony, of Uptown, notes:

> Before moving to Uptown, I had really heard good things about her on the South Side. She was for people who were low income and the homeless and everybody. But moving there I just said, oh, no. This is unacceptable. You know, it wasn't that there were one or two homeless people in my back yard or up and down the street. There were seven in the alley every night.
>
> And then there was a machine made out of that. So you have the social services, you have these transitional housing and low income housing, really dense, and you have the social services, so you had this whole mechanism for getting votes out. It's a machine. It's legitimate. It worked. However, who does it work for?

I found very few Shiller supporters among the active residents I interviewed for this book. Shiller announced in 2010 that she would not seek re-election in 2011.

The other large, active organization is the Organization of the Northeast (ONE), which not only encompasses Uptown but also Rogers Park, Edgewater, and Ravenswood, the community directly west of Uptown. ONE's stated mission is toward "Building a successful multi-ethnic, mixed-economic community on the northeast side of Chicago, in the neighborhoods of Uptown, Edgewater, Rogers Park and Ravenswood" (ONE 2009). ONE, according to Maly, "worked for decades advocating for low-income residents and ensuring that affordable housing remained available in Uptown. By the 1990s, ONE . . . had become less anti-development than they were in the 1970s, although they remained [a] reasonably strong grassroots organization dedicated to stopping or slowing gentrification in Uptown" (2006, 72). Maly credits their work with the maintenance of diversity in Uptown, but residents I spoke to in this study were, without exception, critical of their work, feeling that they were firmly anti-development and pro-Shiller. Several participants told stories of being verbally and publicly attacked for taking a stance that differed from ONE's, even if carefully measured and offering alternative ways to maintain diversity.

While I did speak to some residents active in these organizations, the majority of residents I spoke with in Uptown were not closely connected to either the UCC or ONE, but rather to their small, local block clubs, which differed from Edgewater's large and well-networked block clubs and Rogers Park's mostly inactive block clubs. Some Uptown block clubs included exactly one block, or were otherwise very tightly confined geographically. I began to think of Uptown as a collection of micro-communities—each organized around a small geographical space or a very specific political issue (such as the development of Wilson Yard, a formerly desolate site that has since redeveloped into a site with both a Target and subsidized housing, or opposing the redevelopment of a specific building) rather than an umbrella community like Edgewater. While these micro-communities are aware of, and speak freely about, the larger organizations of UCC or ONE, their active participation most often did not formally link to them.

These community divisions aside, today Uptown is widely regarded as one of the most diverse communities in the city, and at least through the 2000 Census it had retained its status as stably diverse. Table 1.3 provides a breakdown of Uptown's racial demographics in the 1980, 1990, and 2000 census. In 1990 the median income in Uptown was $26,328 and in 2000 the median income was $32,368 (Chicago Fact Finder 2009). The percentage of rental housing in Uptown was 85.6 percent in 1990 and 77.4 percent in 2000 (Chicago Fact Finder 2009). While there has been concern about gentrification in the years since 2000, the community is still perceived as racially and economically diverse by its residents. Indeed, a recent study used a composite measure of multiple diversity scales (centered around ethnicity, age, and income) and found Uptown to be the most diverse in Chicago (Fischer & Schweitzerman 2008).

Table 1.3. Uptown Racial Diversity 1980–2000

Percent of Total	White	Black	Latino	Asian
1980	47	15	24	11
1990	39	24	23	14
2000	42	21	20	13

Source: US Census

Now that I have introduced the communities themselves, it should be noted that in the chapters that follow, when I quote residents whom I interviewed for this project, I will be giving them a gendered pseudonym to protect their identity. For that same reason, I do not list their racial identity. While most of the residents that I interviewed are white, a topic I discuss further in chapters 2 and 5, about 25 percent were not white. Given the close networks in these communities, and the relatively low numbers of racial minorities in each, naming one's race with their neighborhood could compromise the anonymity of residents of color. Further, while the communities are distinct, my analysis of the interview data, and my experiences with the residents, did not reveal any striking differences between communities when it came to their discussions of race and diversity, nor in the types of community action surrounding those issues. As such, they are treated in most of this book as an integrated whole.

AMBIVALENCE AND PRIDE

The larger goal of this book is to understand how limited tools for understanding and discussing the significance of race and racism in contemporary American society creates limited action around diversity. This is the ambivalence expressed in the title of the book. In many ways it stems from contradictory aims. Residents are both color-blind and pro-diversity. That is, they hold to the tenets of color-blind ideologies, as I explore in chapter 3, and yet adhere to a positive discourse around diversity, as I explore in chapter 4. Both of those discourses exist alongside a deep ambivalence around matters of race, class, development, safety, education, and community. This ambivalence sits alongside their pride in their community as diverse spaces, and reveal, I think, the larger anxieties and ambivalence around race in the contemporary United States.

Despite those limitations, however, there is both hope and possibility. There is hope in the desires and intentions of the committed, active residents in these communities, whose thoughts and energies are laid out in the pages that follow. Further, there is possibility in the structures, efforts, and challenges that communities like these face. While there is ambivalence, there is still pride. And where there is pride, there is something to be learned.

2

ACTIVE RESIDENTS AND THEIR WORK

These stably racially diverse communities would not exist without the efforts of the committed residents living within them. Not everyone is interested and willing to live in a racially diverse community, let alone in actively working to shape it. This chapter "introduces" those who are, even as I conceal their identity for their privacy and protection. In this chapter I provide some detail about the participants whose voices fill this book, what prompted their involvement in their community, and the types of community projects that these residents have undertaken to improve their neighborhoods.

Reading about these forms of community action and the demographics of the people I interviewed for this book provides important context for the chapters that will follow. Most of this book is devoted to the negotiations that take place between the ideal of diversity and color-blind society and the very real context of a racially diverse urban community. Better understanding the people whose voices I will be analyzing later in the book, and the projects that they are working to support, gives their race talk concrete meaning. It helps us see the very real dilemmas that they face when working to reconcile competing values and goals in their community.

MEET THE PARTICIPANTS

For the research that went into this book, I interviewed 41 people who live and are active in shaping these communities. Twelve of those people were residents of Rogers Park, 17 were residents of Edgewater, and 12 were Uptown residents. My strategy was to speak to as many people who were active in these communities as possible, but I allowed the residents in the community to define what "active" meant. Had I put confines around the term, I may have missed the range of involvement that I explore later in this chapter, all of which matter in the overall shape of the community.

Further, these communities are very well networked. Especially within each community, but in many cases even between them, these residents know one another precisely because they are the ones who attend the community meetings, work actively with the aldermen, attend and in fact create community-wide events, and otherwise get around the community. In fact, when I interviewed some of these folks in public places like a coffee shop, restaurant, or bar, we were without fail interrupted by people who knew them, and talk would inevitably rove to the current community issue or next community event. This allowed me in turn to meet more people.

My strategy from a research perspective was to conduct snowball sampling. Living in Edgewater, I happened to know or be otherwise connected to a number of active people in each of the three communities, and I began there. By the end of the year in which I conducted this research, from late 2007 until late 2008, few new names were being suggested to me. This made me feel satisfied that I had sufficiently tapped the network and talked to most of the community's active residents. While a few passed on the opportunity for an interview or were otherwise wary of participating in the project, the vast majority were quick to agree to an interview and otherwise embraced my project. Several residents took a very active role in helping me recruit participants, introducing me in person, by phone, or by email to a large number of other residents in their community. Several others embraced my work by using the interview not just as a chance for me to collect my data, but also as an opportunity to educate me about the work, the history, and the commitment of the community on a range of issues. Those folks gave or showed me a number of pamphlets, photos, maps, and other artifacts which not only enriched my data and our interview, but my understanding of and appreciation for the work being done in these communities.

Although you will "meet" many of the residents through the pseudonym I have given them as you read this book, it is worth understanding their characteristics as a group. This section highlights what I think are the most important elements of residents' social identities, things like their race and gender and homeowner status which deeply impact their experiences in the community and their motivations to become involved, which I discuss later in this chapter. While the focus of my book is primarily the racial dynamics of these diverse communities, our statuses and experiences are always shaped by a matrix of identities, patterned by social inequalities. That is, the experience of whites in this community will be in part shared based on their racial privilege, but also stratified by class, gender, sexual orientation, etc. The same is true for people of color.

While there are active black, Asian, and Latina/o residents whose voices appear in this book, my primary analysis is on the color line between whites and people of color. I also only identify participants by a gendered pseudonym and their neighborhood when I quote them in this book. While this may seem counterintuitive given my focus on racial dynamics, there are so few people of color involved in these communities that providing a race, gender, and community name could compromise the confidentiality that I promised as part of my research design. So, to use a hypothetical example, were I to refer to a Latina in Rogers Park, even by pseudonym, most active residents in the community would easily be able to figure out who I am quoting. Chapter 5 is devoted entirely to the issue of one's racial identity in the community, and there the race of the residents will be more explicit. But for the rest of the book, I describe the person speaking by neighborhood and a gendered pseudonym only.

As noted above, despite these being racially diverse communities, the majority of active residents in this study and in these communities are white. This was to the dismay of most of the residents I interviewed. As John, of Edgewater, said, "To be frank, I've constantly talked about the fact that, for the most part, when I would go to these meetings, it was white people, it was primarily older white people." This is likely related to the fact that the majority of active residents are also homeowners. Lakeside Community Development Corporation, an organization that works to preserve affordable housing in Rogers Park, conducted a study in 2006 and identified a disproportionate number of white homeowners and white high-income earners in Rogers Park.

My experience in the community, and the community race and income numbers in chapter 1, indicate that Edgewater and Uptown are no different than Rogers Park in this regard. That is, it is the white residents who are most likely in these communities to have the wealth or income to purchase a home. Further, researchers have demonstrated that homeownership impacts community involvement (see Krysan 2002; Oliver 2000). About half of the residents spoke about home ownership being an impetus for their neighborhood work. Interestingly, some spoke about this as almost a standard sort of answer either in their tone or in their wording, indicating that this reason was either common among new homeowners or something that they had seen repeatedly in the course of their community involvement. When I asked Denise how she first got involved in Edgewater, she said matter-of-factly, "Because I was now a homeowner, and I wanted to assist with improving the quality of life in the neighborhood." More analysis of residents' motivations for community involvement are found later in this chapter.

With more whites owning property in these diverse communities, and more property owners likely to become actively involved in community politics and other forms of social action, the majority who then shape the community are the white homeowners. In fact, although it is not a 1-1 mapping, the same number of residents are white as are homeowners among the residents in this book.

Note again, however, that this is the trend and not the rule. I interviewed a small number of white renters and property owners who are people of color for this book.

Table 2.1. Participants' Racial Identity

	Whites	People of Color
Rogers Park	10	2
Edgewater	11	6
Uptown	9	3
Total	30	11

Table 2.2. **Participants' Housing Status**

	Own Property	Rent
Rogers Park	8	4
Edgewater	14	3
Uptown	8	4
Total	30	11

John's comment above about community meetings being populated by "primarily older white people" also seems accurate to me. The youngest people I interviewed and who were identified as active community members were in their late 20s. Note that while there are several schools and universities in these communities with politically active students, at the time of my interviews none were identified as active in the community politics per se. It is likely that this approach misses a population that is not only politically active but also strongly supportive of diversity initiatives. However, since the implications of this book are mostly tied to the maintenance of diversity within the communities, a transient population like students is unlikely to have a legitimate and lasting role in shaping the community's diversity beyond the universities' steady supply of student populations.

Most, as table 2.3 indicates, were middle aged, likely a factor related to their home or career status. I did not ask residents I interviewed their age, but many revealed their age without my asking. When they did not do so, I am comfortable inferring their age based on their appearance and some other clues such as time in the community relative to school or career. Therefore, while it may not be perfectly accurate, I feel very comfortable breaking down the residents into the age categories below.

Men and women were relatively evenly spread, as indicated in table 2.4, with only slightly more men than women participating actively in the communities. Gender at times will impact my analysis of residents'

Table 2.3. **Participants' Age**

	20s–30s	40s–60s	70+
Rogers Park	3	8	1
Edgewater	0	15	2
Uptown	2	8	2
Total	5	31	5

Table 2.4. Participants' Gender

	Men	Women
Rogers Park	5	7
Edgewater	11	6
Uptown	7	5
Total	23	18

activity; again the gender is reflected in the pseudonym I chose for residents whom I quote in this book. None of the residents self-identified as transgender, and all gender categories were inferred by self-presentation and name.

I did ask everyone how long they had lived in the community at some point in the interview; those results appear in table 2.5. Their answers here were relatively evenly spread, with the lowest at two years and the highest who have lived there 30 years or more, including some lifetime residents. The average tenure in the community among residents was about 15 years, but with such a wide spread of data, the reasons for involvement likely have little to do with time in the community. I discuss those factors and motivations later in this chapter.

Finally, the remaining tables offer some demographic snapshots of participants' sexual identity and political views. These were not things I asked participants to reveal; rather they emerged on their own, were inferred by observation of artifacts in their home or on their body, or were gleaned from references that were made to policies or experiences at various junctures in the interview. I inferred political views based on direct disclosure, political paraphernalia (as my interviews were conducted in the height of the 2008 election), discussion of local and national political figures, or other elements of political discourse. While the data in tables 2.6 and 2.7 may not be precise, they do provide a rough and important picture of both factors among the community's active residents.

Table 2.5. Participants' Tenure in the Community

	1–10 years	11–20 years	21–30 years	30+ years
Rogers Park	6	3	2	1
Edgewater	6	5	4	2
Uptown	6	3	1	2
Total	18	11	7	5

Table 2.6.   Participants' Political Views

	Libertarian	Conservative	Moderate	Liberal	Progressive
Rogers Park	0	0	1	7	4
Edgewater	0	0	5	11	1
Uptown	1	0	5	6	0
Total	1	0	11	24	5

The political views of the active residents have a special significance in the chapter on color-blind racial ideology that follows. As table 2.6 indicates, these active residents are not just overwhelmingly liberal, but so are the identities of the communities themselves. This is perhaps especially true for Rogers Park, home to Heartland Café, a restaurant and bar with an attached store that proudly proclaims its progressive politics. However, all communities are known to be liberal communities. Edgewater contains Andersonville, which is home to many proud gay and lesbian residents and business owners, and Uptown's alderman from 1987–2011 was Helen Shiller, a Democrat whom many identify with progressive politics.

The communities are also known to be home to or welcoming of diverse sexual identities. The sexual identities of the residents I interviewed are presented in table 2.7. I spoke to several gays and lesbians in the course of this study—many who were out and expressed their sexual identity to me in the course of the interview. Others were otherwise out, as other residents spoke about another resident's sexual identity in passing or relative to a specific issue. As with politics and gender, there will be times in the chapters which follow that discussion of sexual identity is important for my analysis. However, only residents that self-disclosed as gay or lesbian are identified as such in this book.

As this section illustrates, the people I interviewed for this book are a relatively diverse group who are working to sustain and improve a very diverse community. While the majority are white homeowners, their

Table 2.7.   Participants' Sexual Identities

	Gay or Lesbian	Heterosexual
Rogers Park	1	11
Edgewater	7	10
Uptown	2	10
Total	10	31

interest in the community is not exclusively one of self-interest. As this book reveals, they take pride in their diverse community and work to promote and sustain it in complex and yet committed ways. While diversity is not always their chief goal, their respect for and pride in these communities runs deep in their discourse and in their social action. Their commitment to their communities is, in large part, what makes them such attractive places to live.

WHAT MAKES A COMMUNITY ACTIVIST?

After meeting the residents whose thoughts and experiences are detailed in this book, it is worth considering how they are able to become involved in their communities in the first place. Certainly more people would like to be connected to their neighbors and involved in their communities than are able to do so. I find that those who do have some combination of character, time, and commitment that either first brought them into this unpaid community work or otherwise structures their commitments. Each, as I detail below, also reveal more about the dynamics of these communities and the power relations within.

Character

Calling the first of three loci for community action character is not meant to be pejorative. Rather, it speaks to the sense that some have of themselves, or a consistent track record, of being "community people." About a quarter of the 41 people I interviewed discussed personal histories of community engagement or political involvement before moving into Rogers Park, Edgewater, or Uptown. They are the type of person who finds and connects with their local community no matter where they are living, and did so quite intentionally upon moving into their Chicago community.

When they moved to Rogers Park, Edgewater, or Uptown, they looked for block club or community council information and immediately began going to meetings. Carla, of Edgewater, responded to my question about what prompted her to first get involved as follows:

> Just being in the community. I'm an easy sell when it comes to that. I will seek out what's in the area just because I think you need to be involved. So I saw a flyer, actually, and talked to a neighbor and said, so what's going on around here? Oh, we have a block club; we have meetings. I'm like, ooh, I want to go. And I went.

Carla also discussed her long history of involvement in other communities around the nation where she had lived before. Her commitment to community as a principle is strong. Lance, also of Edgewater, is another prime example of this type of commitment: "Um, I came back [from overseas] and I really did have a sense of, you know, I want to become more involved in the political process and within the community."

Even without a personal history like Carla's or Lance's, about half of the people I interviewed went on to speak at some point about the importance they place on civic engagement. They spoke emphatically about the moral impetus to participate in one's community, parents who had inspired them through their own civic engagement, and a desire to give back to their communities. They acknowledged that community is something that takes work, time, and energy, and understand that this is difficult to sustain. Despite a concurrent admission of feeling burned out at times and uncertain about how long they will be able to last, this civic engagement and the positives gleaned from their involvement have thus far sustained them and their work in the community.

For others, drive toward involvement was simply a heartfelt desire to set down roots, to know people in the community, and to, as one Rogers Park resident, Shannon, so memorably put it, "Learn what it means to be a good neighbor." Similarly, five became involved simply because they had gotten to know so many people in their neighborhood or had seen others' involvement and decided to become active as a result. Notably, they have remained involved even if this first contact happened years ago. This sense of character that I've described here was palpable when I met the active residents. Their commitment to community, civic engagement, and neighborhood networking is a central piece of who they are as people.

Time

Of course, there may be many more out there with these ideals, but
without the time or energy to be involved. Lucy, of Edgewater, was
discussing participation in her block club, and said:

> I'm just looking at their faces going, oh, yeah, retiree, retiree. Oh, uh, uh,
> someone that works at home. Uh, somebody else that owns properties
> and doesn't have a job. Uh, people with flexible time, I guess. They're the
> ones that are active. . . . I notice people with children don't go to block
> club meetings.

Lucy's comments perfectly capture all the dynamics I heard in residents' abilities to be actively involved in their community.

I spoke to only three people, two men and one woman, who were parents of small children. Only one person had kids in high school. Roughly
one third of the 41 residents I interviewed live alone, and indeed named
such freedom from needing to negotiate family schedules as a prime
reason why they were able to devote time to their community. Those
who are now empty nesters spoke of their child-rearing years as a time
when their community involvement lapsed or decreased, in favor of
school involvement and family activities that took them outside of the
community. None of the residents I spoke to sent their children to the
local public schools. Instead they were able to place them in magnet
schools in other parts of the city, opted for private school, or planned
to move to another community when they had school-age children. The
matter of schooling is of critical importance for the families in these
communities, and for the future of diverse communities generally. Prior
research utilizing in-depth interviews in several regions of the country
has demonstrated the centrality of race, and in particular homogenous
whiteness, in parents' determination of what makes "good" schools and
"good" communities (Johnson & Shapiro 2003). Thus, it is not only the
schedule of raising school-age children that structured their involvement, but the racial composition of the diverse schools themselves.

Work also played a critical role in participants' availability. Five of
the 41 were unemployed, several due to the economic crisis, at the
time that I spoke to them. Others began their community engagement
during a time of unemployment or changes in their employment situ-

ation. Another five began or increased their community involvement upon retirement. In fact, one resident spoke of this as an ongoing joke between himself and a recently retired colleague in the community, who had promised to not become an "all-day e-mailer" who is otherwise impatient with those whose schedules don't look like his own. As their joke reveals, some who were working full time expressed mild frustrations with those whose work schedules allowed for near-full time community work.

> It can be hard when so-and-so is home all day and can fire off 20 emails and create their little flyers or whatever they can, and I'm juggling a conference call, at meetings somewhere else downtown, and planning to travel next week. (John, Edgewater)

While I did hear this sentiment echoed several times among participants, this frustration was without fail tempered with an appreciation for their neighbor's work and awareness that everyone does the best they can with the time they have. In fact, full-time workers often said they wish they had the time that those who could be home all day, particularly those who were retired, had.

Like John above, about a third of the people I interviewed work full-time jobs outside the home and have family members or partners who live with them and also compete for their time. These dozen or so people attend numerous block club meetings, community council meetings, CAPS meetings, planning and zoning meetings, safety walks, and block club parties. They also spend their time and energy meeting individually with staff at various political organizations, writing and reading emails, putting together newsletters, distributing leaflets, canvassing local businesses, planting gardens, picking up trash, and getting to know other community members on an individual basis. While they are often tired, these residents remained tireless in their commitment to the sustenance and betterment of their communities.

Commitment

Given the pressures on active residents' time and energy I was, and remain, appreciative of their willingness to fit me into their schedule.

But I also noticed that for about a quarter of the residents, speaking to me wasn't just about helping me with this research, but also itself a form of community involvement. Five residents sat down with me armed with flyers, maps, studies, newsletters, project plans, and other artifacts of their past and continued involvement. In some cases they provided me with copies of these materials, but most often these papers sat ready at kitchen tables for us to examine as we spoke. One resident turned our interview into a sales pitch for his current project, and while graciously answering my questions, also wanted to ask me about whom I might know who could get involved in their projects, or invite out to the next community event. While these examples are among the most overt, they represent the strain of commitment that also helped me understand what makes a community activist.

About a quarter of the residents also asked me somewhere during the course of the interview how my project might serve a practical purpose for them in the community, and on that basis were very generous in sharing information about their networks and suggestions for other participants with me. I had the sense that these same residents claimed my project through their participation, with the hope that my work would produce something useful for them. The generosity, time, and networks that these busy people, already doing so much for the community, shared with me was humbling. My hope is that this book, and especially its conclusion, will highlight what they are doing right and provide suggestions for ways to better move forward in the future.

This tangible commitment to organizing and the strategies involved in community activism are hallmark of the people I met while conducting interviews for this book. For 5 of the 41, a specific issue piqued their interest and got them out to a meeting. In these cases, their sustained involvement thereafter is worth noting. As mentioned above, active residents spoke about widespread community involvement dropping off after a particular safety or development issue had been resolved. Instead, these folks continued their community involvement beyond that first issue, and have remained involved ever since.

Another five spoke similarly about the need for some type of community structure or process which had not been in place before, or which had become ineffective. They talked about chaos, dysfunction, conflict, or stagnation that was inhibiting the ability of residents to best respond to an issue. They undertook, often with others who named the same problems, the task of setting up new or reinvigorating old structures in the community. Lance, of Edgewater, is a good example of these types of responses:

> Um, we had a local issue that deals with that building that was built right over there on [a street] in our local block club, and there was kind of a power vacuum in our block club; there was really no leadership. And I kinda took up the mantle of doing this, and it . . . and that's how I really became involved locally, in this community, as a block club president.

These stories were certainly more conflict-ridden than the other types of responses, yet their comments remained polite and measured. There was some frustration with some individuals who had blocked this process in the past and who in some cases remained barriers for community work. In three instances, situations like this created something of a dividing line, with competing block clubs or organizations working in defiance of one another, effectively forcing others who might become involved to choose between them. However, in most cases the new block club or new community structure entirely replaced the other without much confusion or contention.

About three quarters of residents I spoke to, in all three neighborhoods, were in some way or another connected to their local block club. For roughly three quarters of the residents I met, joining their block club was their entrée into active community involvement. For about ten of these residents, community issues were also directly ones of either service or social justice. While many of these residents were also linked in to their local block clubs or other community structures, their motivations for getting involved included a desire to contribute to charity or service programs in the community. These programs typically were geared toward teens, the poor, the elderly, immigrants, and renters. For three, this was tied to their faith. For five this was more closely tied to their political beliefs, and for two it was a moral aspect of their civic participation. In the words of Larry, when discussing his involvement in the Civil Rights Movement, "It just seemed morally right. It was just right. It was just—some things you just know in your core that it's the right thing to do." Within this category about half were younger and channeling their political beliefs into local avenues, and the other half were strongly influenced by coming of age during, or for some, actively participating in, the Civil Rights Movement.

As one might expect in the context of competing demands and the commitment to strong ideals of service and community, burnout was a serious risk. More than half of the people I interviewed discussed dealing with burnout at one time or another. In some cases, someone else's burnout was the impetus for participants' own active community involvement: a block club had lapsed into oblivion and was no longer active because someone had gotten tired and given up, or a long-time leader was actively seeking new participation because she was nearing burnout and wanted fresh ideas and support. It is also revealing that about a quarter of the residents spoke with ambivalence about their community involvement. Their sense of civic responsibility kept them hard at work on the community's issues, but in a more perfect world they would be spending more time in their gardens, relaxing on their porches, or at local restaurants and bars than at planning and zoning committee meetings, low-turnout block club events, or the alderman's office.

This ambivalence was particularly pronounced when residents identified a common trend: getting bodies at block club meetings was easy when there was a real or perceived problem in the neighborhood, but difficult when other, less active residents didn't feel personally impacted by community efforts. Active residents sometimes grumbled about their neighbors wanting to constantly be updated and given information, but rarely doing the long and often tedious work of collecting and disseminating such information. Kurt, of Uptown, noted:

> But now if you were to suddenly say to people over there, we're going to change the flow of traffic on one of these streets because we're tired of all this cutting around Foster by going down this street, oh, you can bet people are going to be out left and right. And if there's a proposal to tell them that they've got to lose seven parking spaces on the street, oh no, they'll be up in arms. But get them out there to talk about a winter clothing drive or a holiday party that involves going to [a local social service organization] to do it, oh, you won't, no. There's just no way. People are just, no.

Kurt laughed, as did many others, when they spoke about this common problem. But with this laughter residents spoke also about their own resilience in the face of burnout or fatigue. The well-being of the community, at least during the moment when I spoke to them, remained as important as their own energy and time. In fact, many have been able to maintain their involvement for years.

FOUR TYPES OF COMMUNITY ACTION

As discussed in chapter 1, my strategy in interviewing residents was to focus specifically on their involvement in their communities, rather than asking abstract questions about how they value or define diversity. For that reason, I got to learn in-depth about the impressive extent and range of involvement for all of the active residents in this book. Based on my coding of this interview data, I divided the scope of activities I heard about from participants into four major categories: social, safety, development, and justice. While there were several types of projects taking place in each category, the largest number of projects, and the greatest extent of community involvement, fell into the safety and development categories. These same categories are the ones residents in these communities also identified as the "hot button" issues, the type that are most contested, and the type that draws the most interest and participation from fellow community members.

Safety

Safety constituted one of the biggest categories of community involvement. Safety issues were often an impetus for community involvement, as a spike in crime or specific concerns about safety in the community often pulled people out to meetings for the first time. Although it varies by neighborhood, with Uptown being the most heavily dominated by safety-related organizing among participants in this study, followed by Edgewater and then Rogers Park, each of these communities have collectively faced the issue of safety in significant ways.

It is worth noting that, despite some common perceptions, each of these three communities is a relatively safe place to live and spend time. During the year that I conducted the bulk of my interviews, 2008, Rogers Park, Edgewater, and Uptown fell at or below citywide averages for index crimes, violent crime, aggravated assault, and homicide (Chicago Police Department 2009). Further, crime has itself has been steadily declining in the city of Chicago (Chicago Police Department 2007). Most community members know this, and some like Tom, of Uptown, actively work to educate fellow community members as well as the general public about the relative safety of these communities:

> . . . Look at the statistics. We have one of the lowest crime rates in the city of Chicago. We are in the bottom 20 to 10 percent for about every single crime in the city of Chicago.
>
> You can go on, you know, what is it, the ICAM reports. Then you can go to the Chicago Police Department, and they have statistics, so I'm always sending those out in emails. Yeah, I know you saw this guy, but look, this is what's really happening. We have one of the lowest incidents of shootings. We have one of the lowest incidents of this.
>
> I always point out to people you're more likely to get mugged or raped in Lakeview than here in Uptown. It's more likely your car's going to get broken into, your apartment, your condo's going to get broken into. We have very, very low crime.

Sentiments like Tom's are important to recognize, as it affirms residents' commitment to their community in responsible and informed ways. It also contextualizes the work that they are doing in these communities to ensure continued safety or in many cases make these communities even more safe. With few exceptions, the majority of the residents I spoke to were not motivated by fear. While later chapters explore some of the ways that these perceptions and concerns are racialized, it is important to recognize that most residents of these communities are making an effort to accurately understand the safety issues in their community and respond in ways that are both effective and just.

One of the most creative strategies I heard about in my conversations with active residents in these communities was a coordinated network of neighborhood walks. While safety-driven neighborhood walks are in themselves nothing new (see Wegener 1979), the level of organization and commitment that the residents in Uptown have coordinated is remarkable. Anthony, of Edgewater, reflected back on the early years of this organization: "So we had, for several years, positive loitering marches, and we're taking back the park. Marches and community effort to watch the park and walk our dogs in the park and get rid of the gang dealers [sic]." Walter, of Uptown, explained this strategy as follows:

> And, uh, so we set up a watch, and get involved with the [block], which has been very successful. Actually, we were out there for about six days. A lotta activity. Uh, gang members out on the other side of [the street]. You could see drug deals. Call 911. It was busy, and we were out there from 10:00 to 11:00. Seventh day, and then I got another block club down, so we have, uh, from [one major street to another] covered with the groups standing at the end. It just went dead. And it's held that way now, and we're only out once a week. Uh, and it's a good example where, if people stand up, the bad guys'll move away.

Others whom I interviewed in this same area of Uptown have confirmed the palpable decline in gang activity since the walks have commenced.

That strategy of community policing is perhaps most famously manifest in the CAPS program. CAPS is the acronym for the Chicago Alternative Policing Strategy, a program which began in Chicago in 1993 as a means of engaging local communities not just in responding to crime but also in identifying local crime issues. According to the City of Chicago's website, "Problem solving at the neighborhood level is supported by a variety of strategies, including neighborhood-based beat officers; regular Beat Community Meetings involving police and residents; extensive training for both police and community; more efficient use of City services that impact crime; and new technology to help police and residents target crime hot spots" (City of Chicago, 2009). It should be noted that a recent study has identified CAPS as a tool increasingly being utilized by wealthier white residents, making the context in which this community tool has a direct relationship to the maintenance of the communities' diversity palpable (Nyden, Edlynn, and Davis 2006, 16–19).

CAPS involvement was common among residents I spoke to, particularly in Uptown and Edgewater. Many residents not only regularly attended CAPS meetings but also have taken on an additional role with local police by researching and reporting area crime issues. Some have become court advocates, helping to document and witness the implementation of justice at the level of the courts. This requires a considerable amount of education and effort. One resident showed me detailed maps of specific gang areas that he uses in his work with the police and courts. Gathering and using this information was critical in empowering community members. It made them engaged and informed participants in struggles to contain crime rather than passive recipients of crime. This enabled them to neither overreact to the reality of crime in these communities nor stand by helplessly as crime took place. Police roll calls were also empowering, as revealed by Eric, in Edgewater:

> I was at a . . . they do a roll call. . . . They do an open roll call right . . . in the middle of the neighborhood, you know, their change of shifts, and squad cars going from every different direction, you know, and call the officers by name, and they update on what's going on.

The effectiveness of these roll calls is not empirically demonstrated, but like the coordinated walks and "positive loitering," they are strongly supported and attended by members of the community, and felt to be very effective in symbolically standing up to crime and reasserting their control over the neighborhood.

That is not to say that some residents did not feel as though they were under assault. Several residents of Uptown in particular spoke of feelings of combat, fatigue, and even shock as they either first acclimated to the neighborhood or remained in it despite near-constant problems of crime nearby. Calling 911 became a routine practice as residents witnessed drug deals or violent assaults on their block. For some, they lived in the communities during a time when this was happening on a daily basis, and in response some organized phone trees in hopes that multiple 911 calls would effectively capture police attention. One resident spoke of death threats, not to him but to a neighbor, in response to this activity, as their efforts had been effective enough to stifle gang activity.

Unfortunately, at times some of the residents of these communities have been victims of crime. It was most often the longtime residents who told stories of being burglarized or mugged. Yet they did not pack the moving van and leave the community like many others did at the time. Without fail, they spoke instead of a certainty that the crime would decrease, the neighborhood would improve, and that in general things would get better. Margaret, of Uptown, said, "And it was pretty bad there for a while, now that would be, that would have been—that would have been '70s. It was bad. I mean, needles in the alley, and lots of bad stuff over there." I asked her if she considered leaving during that time. "We really didn't. We really didn't. We knew it would change. We knew it would, you know. Those people come and go. They don't stay. And, ah, it's much better now."

Given my method of speaking to active residents in these communities, I was unable to hear the voices of those who did chose to leave the community. But I did hear some stories about them along the way:

> Um, a lotta neighbors have moved. One of my neighbors moved, when he was coming home—He was coming home from work at 6:15 on a night like tonight, and was parking the car, 'cause they didn't have a garage. And there was gunfire, and it was, like, right where that window was, shooting past him. He went in the house, told his wife, "Honey, there was gunfire 20 feet from me."
>
> And [she] said, "That's it. The house goes on the market tomorrow." They were gonna wait until their son was about three and a half before they were gonna move, you know, for schools. And that was it. They were gone. And that was, like, a year and a half ago. Gone. They were gone four months later.—Susan, Uptown

Susan's comments reveal not only the persistence of those that choose to stay, but once again the strategy on the part of many parents to leave the community once their children reach school age. Many parents in prior studies tie this concretely to fear of crime. As Johnson and Shaprio have demonstrated, even among parents committed to diversity and equality, "despite their desire to be 'part of the solution,' they will become part of what they themselves identify as 'the problem' of racism and residential segregation" (2003, 184). With that choice comes the perpetuation of structural inequalities favoring whites.

Other strategies related to crime included working with aldermen to alter or remove physical structures that residents had identified as sites of crime. In some cases this was directly tied to the next section on development, as residents perceive that absentee landlords and abandoned buildings are strongly correlated to criminal activity. In other cases this meant removing things like newspaper boxes that were being used as benches or depositories among people who had not been identified as members of the community. At the time of my research in 2008,

Edgewater residents were encouraging one another, through the block club network, to display their address in the back of their property, so that police could better respond to incidents that took place in the alleys. Finally, block club email networks constantly inform residents about recent incidents and strategies to protect one's self against such crimes.

Development

The next major category of community action is development. Like many urban communities, the histories of Rogers Park, Edgewater, and Uptown are histories of contested development. This is true from their early days as either administrative or de facto suburbs for Chicago's wealthy elite, through their various reputations as sites of decay and desolation, and up to today's concern over gentrification. This section will explore some of the history that is still unfolding for the active residents in this book, as they debate the future of development in their communities.

At the time that I was conducting research for this book, each of the three communities had at least one major site that was being debated among community residents. In Rogers Park, residents were concerned about the area north of Howard, which is a struggling commercial district with a large number of vacant lots and rental units that accept housing vouchers. In Edgewater, the development of a 12-story condo building with vast retail space in the bottom level was a site of contention, as residents worried about increased density and expressed disappointment that the retailer was Aldi instead of their desired Trader Joe's. Edgewater has also long been concerned with the Winthrop-Kenmore Corridor, once known as Arson Alley, the strip of mostly rental housing where I lived during my six years in the community, and where there is both a legacy of absentee landlords and a perception of crime. In Uptown, the debate centered around the development of Wilson Yard, a five acre former rail yard that has since been developed into housing and retail using, in part, TIF (tax increment) funding from the city.

As the above sites reveal, ambivalence often rules when it comes to development. More than three quarters of residents want to see a more vibrant dining, retail, and bar scene to both boost local business infrastructure and invite more interest into these communities. Indeed, this has proven vital in sustaining neighborhoods' diversity (Nyden et al 1998, Ellen 2000). Residents want to be able to patronize local businesses and in some cases even make use of national chains that are to their liking. At the same time, residents are most often wary of two elements that have often accompanied such development—the addition of affordable housing and increased density.

Residents typically do not oppose affordable housing outright. Instead, they worry about the percentage of affordable housing relative to market rate housing, either within a particular new development or within a given locale.

> It's what people are talking about they tried to do with Cabrini-Green, which was to tear down the hundred percent very low income high-rises and build a mixed income community. And that, I think, is very sensible. And in the 1990 census, Uptown was close to 40 percent low income, and that's too much.—Clark, Uptown

The central concern I heard was that a concentration of low-income housing or "Section 8" housing has been proven to be ineffective and unsafe (see Popkin et al 2000; Mitchell 1971).

This assessment has been central for those who oppose the ways in which Uptown's Wilson Yard has been redesigned. Whereas the original plans for Wilson Yard included mixed-income housing, including some housing at market rate, revised plans included 100 percent low-income housing. A website devoted to the cause at the time prominently featured a quote by "Christopher D, Renowned Urban Planner" stating, "Wilson Yard is a future slum for Uptown." Uptown residents have been similarly concerned about the prevalence of scattered-site CHA developments in their community, particularly when they are built in high concentration to one another, making the developments, in their view, anything but scattered.

Edgewater and Rogers Park residents have similar concerns about low-income housing being concentrated in their communities. Studies have shown that concern over affordable housing walks a very careful racial line (Charles 2003; Patillo 2001; Charles 2000), the dynamics of which are explored in later chapters. Residents in Rogers Park, Edgewater, and Uptown work hard to reconcile the realities of housing diversity in their community with a desire to maintain the community's character. They do so while concurrently ensuring their continued safety and attending to the type of development that they feel is beneficial for the community. Because of the weight of these competing forces, issues of affordable or public housing remain central sites of debate and ambivalence.

Public housing sites are not the only ones that motivate concerns about density. Residents were also concerned about the density of market-rate housing, which impacts traffic, parking, noise, light, and litter. Community members actively organized around density issues, most often when new construction was proposed. Most often the avenue for this organization was linked to the community approval structure of the 48th Ward at the time. The alderman of that ward, Mary Ann Smith, had retained a model that her predecessor created whereby community representatives (namely block club representatives but also some community organizations) vote on all matters related to zoning and planning. Mary Ann Smith's website listed examples of these matters as follows: "zoning changes and variances; PPA [Public Place for Amusement] licenses; public development funding, etc." (M. Smith 2009). Residents report that Alderman Smith responded to the community's desires on almost all of these decisions. There were dissenters, but as John, of Edgewater, notes:

> Well, I think one of the things is we're fortunate, politics aside, that Alderman Smith listens to her community organizations. So I do think that ECC and the block clubs have had great success in being heard. I don't think she necessarily always does what we say, but that's what we elect her for, so I don't see that as a fault. Others might. But I think she does look for community involvement.

Franklin, of Edgewater, put the process in a larger context:

> So sometimes I think that the alderman should make good, hard decisions, what's best for the entire community and not be so tied to this group of 35 voices. . . . It's not a perfect system, and I don't know how you could make it a perfect system, I mean, unless you give every single person a vote on every single issue. But there's 65,000 residents in Edgewater, and 64,000, in my opinion, don't care.

Another common element of development-related organization in these communities was an effort to make the communities "green." In some ways, the push for green communities is an extension of a commitment to "beautify" the communities, a decades-long project in all three communities (see Edgewater Community Council 1986). Both "greening" and "beautifying" are in some way inherently tied to the livability of the community. Residents also describe both efforts as "nonconfrontational." Many have been involved with gardening projects that transformed either a barren concrete space or a neglected public park into a community garden, a place for art, or a more pleasant place to walk. Residents described this as difficult work, but also enjoyable, as they literally got their hands dirty and along the way spent social time getting to know their neighbors and learning more about the community. Some of the difficulty also lied in the upkeep or at times outright destruction of such projects. Plants were sometimes torn up; art was sometimes covered with graffiti; and plants along a busy road were often in need of regular cleaning and revival.

While the beautification projects and to a lesser extent public art and gardening projects have gone on throughout most of the tenure of residents in these communities, the "green" revolution—a desire to make these communities eco-friendly—is relatively new. This was a common topic of discussion for community members, who have engaged a variety of projects in this arena. There have been many community workshops in recent years about green gardening and green home renovation. There has been a drive to encourage neighbors to use energy efficient bulbs in their porch lights and in their homes. There has been a push to embrace local farmers markets, and to support local businesses who themselves undertake a green initiative, either by growing their own food, having a rooftop garden, or serving as a site for recycling and composting in the community.

One significant element of the green development projects in these communities is the fact that it has become a rare point of contact and cooperation among the three communities. While Rogers Park, Edgewater, and Uptown residents face many of the same concerns about crime, development, transit, housing, and schools, it has been rare that the communities come together to work on these issues. However, environmental issues may be the issue to facilitate this inter-neighbor-hood cooperation.

> The environment's a hot topic everywhere you go. Um, and it's something that's not that controversial. I mean, if we said we were all gonna get together and, uh, band against anti-Semitism, you know. I mean, most people say, oh, I don't know if I want to do that. You know, I-I-I gotta wash my car today, you know.
>
> But the environment. Nobody's gonna say, oh, I, you know, I want to pollute my world, you know. And so it's just—there's not a whole lot of opposition.—Larry, Edgewater

Indeed, scholars have recognized efforts like these as vital in nurturing diverse communities (Ellen 2000; Maly 2006; Nyden et al 1998).

Social

Social events constituted the third category of community involve-ment among residents interviewed for this book. Many discussed social activities in the community somewhat hesitantly, as though they were of less importance than the other issues. Shannon, of Rogers Park, ex-pressed some of this hesitancy, even as she discussed how they can lead to other work:

> I was trying to make this like a neighborhood *association*, but a lot of people aren't interested in that yet. They're mostly interested in plan-ning the block party. So it's . . . great though, we get together—we've gotten together several times now to talk about hot dogs or hamburgers (*laughter*) and these types of things and then . . . other things come up though. So at the end of every one of these meetings inevitably someone says, "Did you hear about this thing that happened in the neighborhood" or "Who are you voting for" or, and so it's a little bit of an expansion into neighborhood issues.

Indeed, most residents who discussed social activities recognized its value in this way.

Likewise, even when not taking place in an organized capacity like a block club party, barbeque, or bar night, many residents spoke about the individual act of introducing themselves to someone on the street as an inherently political act. "Knowing thy neighbor" is a creed to which many in these communities both adhere and advocate.

> I made a determination that I was going to know everybody on my block. And I just started—I'm gonna know every one of them. So anyway, so I'm walking down the street, and I would just make sure that I said hello to everybody, even if it meant standing there and demanding a response, you know. . . . And, uh, I got to know—I literally know everybody in my neighborhood.—Hank, Uptown

The social arena was not just an outlet for social organization. It was also an impetus. Several community members first met members of their community at local cafés or bars, and in that process of making friends came to talk about and organize around national or community issues.

> Honestly what I started to do was I started hanging out at [a local café], which is just down the block. And honestly that became like a community for me. That was the way that I started to connect with the community . . . I think initially, it was just kind of getting to know the counter person. I mean, that was really the first thing. I was there every day. I got to know her. And, um, and then little by little people—especially in the summer. In winter was maybe not quite that much, but in the summer time, you know, when we got to sit outside, you know, more and more people would just talk to me, and I would talk to people. And we'd start to create conversations and, you know, very organic kind of a thing, you know.—Wendy, Rogers Park

It is worth noting that stories like Wendy's only came from Rogers Park residents. This is likely due to Rogers Park's "hippie" reputation, and the existence of some local restaurants or cafés that have long been sites of political discourse and activity in the neighborhood. In Edgewater, there are few comparable bars or cafés frequented only by locals that have the legacy and history in the community on par with its Rogers Park counterparts. I also suspect that this is linked to my analysis of community structure that I detailed earlier. Residents in Rogers Park most often do not utilize the umbrella community structures and block club networks in order to meet and organize together. Rather, Rogers Park's establishments, particularly those with an overtly liberal or community-centered flair, draw individuals to this shared space, which fosters community and at times social action among the regulars.

In the end, far from being somehow superficial or ineffective, social events and social interactions provide one important element of community engagement among these communities' active residents. While the bulk of their time may be spent working on other projects, social events serve the function of networking among neighbors, building trust and community, and fostering involvement in other projects of importance to the community. These informal, nonorganizational associations, or social capital, have been identified as central to such trust (Lowndes 2000; Putnam 2000). Knowing one's neighbor weaves the community members into one another's lives, adding an extra layer of protection, trust, and responsibility to the otherwise institutional protections of policing, governance, and committees.

Justice

The final category of community involvement among the residents I spoke to for this study is that of justice. While issues of safety and development are inherently related to justice in the community, and indeed the site at which most issues of race and diversity are negotiated, there were some elements of community involvement that engaged justice issues outright. This didn't happen often. But it did constitute a distinct category of involvement. For a small number of residents, social justice participation happened as a result of their church. Several churches in the area have either social justice committees or regularly engage justice-related service projects. Typically these organizations or events take on a global justice issue like war or immigration, but often these global themes are considered at least in part with respect to the local community.

Beyond the church context, few residents became involved with organizations with explicitly justice-oriented agendas. There were some, but their involvement was either so instrumental that describing it could imply their identity or so marginal that beyond one event they have had no sustained contact or participation. This is despite the existence of several strong justice-oriented organizations in these communities, who do have a staff and a presence in the community.

One Rogers Park resident, Matthew, discussed what he perceived to be resistance to efforts like this in community beyond the existing community organizations:

> And a lot of people really were kind of resentful for that because I think in Rogers Park there's a real, especially in the white community, which is much more engaged in notions of diversity and inclusion and so on and so forth. I mean, it's much more of a conscious statement from a lot of those folks . . . —people don't want to believe that they're not doing the right thing and that they're not on the right side of the issues. They feel like, well, I moved to Rogers Park because I want to have diversity.
>
> And we would explain that if white families keep moving to Rogers Park for diversity and we're not building any new housing, somebody's got to move out. Well, if the neighborhood was a third, a third, a third, black, white, and Hispanic, and everybody moving in is white . . . And that makes people really uncomfortable.
>
> And we've continued to try to work on issues around diversity and get people to think about what does it mean. We say we like diversity, we're in favor of it, what does that really mean? And what are we doing to defend that? . . . So, I mean, those types of questions I don't think were really being—I'm not aware of those questions being asked in any kind of a systematic fashion. Because no one else is really—I don't hear anyone else really talking about these issues.

Both Matthew's statement and my sampling and observation indicate that beyond the presence of several organizations, the bulk of active community residents are not working on issues of diversity and racial justice directly. Indirect means may still work to sustain the diversity in these communities (Nyden et al 1998; Maly 2006), and this issue is explored in-depth in the final chapter of this book. But the lack of direct effort is important to keep in mind during the following chapters, as it points to a chasm in the community around issues of diversity and social justice.

While there are active bloggers on conservative issues, social justice organizations working on progressive issues, and active residents tied in to various community organizations that are typically liberal, there does not seem to be much contact or involvement between the spheres. Interlaced with the varying community structures in each of the three neighborhoods, and the reality that those who are involved in their communities are often stretched for time and energy, these communities still remain relatively segmented. They are segmented by issue, by social class, by locale, and in some cases also by age, gender, race, and geography. This is true despite the neighborhood's density and diversity. Indeed, nothing guarantees that a diverse community area will not be segregated and segmented within its borders (Farley & Frey 1994; Taylor 1998).

That is not to say that these segments of the neighborhood population resent or willfully avoid one another. Cross-segment talk was in almost all cases respectful, and many community members themselves echoed the reality of all the issues that prevent community coalescence. But as it stands, this is at least one factor inhibiting an intentional organization around social justice and even diversity issues in these communities. While safety and development issues are sites for the negotiation of such issues, to be sure, they have become de facto sites, and as such do not indicate a presence among community members to overtly commit to either a just or a diverse community. Rather, the communities remain largely at the mercy of market forces, competing community concerns, and national ambivalence around race and diversity that I more closely examine in the following chapters.

LIMITATION AND HOPE

This chapter has provided what I hope is an in-depth introduction to the people whose voices appear in the remainder of this book, their motivations for becoming so actively involved in their diverse communities, and the types of activities and involvement that they have pursued. The following chapters reveal the complex web of thought and discussion that takes place around issues of race and diversity in these communities, as these residents work to navigate competing values such as color-blindness and diversity. How does one simultaneously appreciate diversity and argue, using the color-blind frames so prevalent in our society, that race does not matter? How do residents work to develop their communities and support them as diverse places? How do people act meaningfully around issues of crime and safety, while making sense of the race-specific ways that crime is structured and understood? These are not easy challenges to discuss, no less enact.

The next two chapters discuss how residents attempt to do so. Chapter 3 details the extent of color-blind ideologies in these communities. I find that color-blind ideology is still pervasive in these communities, despite their racial diversity and progressive politics. To be sure, it takes a particular liberal flavor—one indicated but not fully explored in previous studies. But it is by no means absent. Active residents are still deeply impacted by, and complicit with, the frames of color-blindness that are so pervasive in the mainstream United States. This chapter also details their strong reliance on coded racial discourse in order to convey racial meaning without directly discussing race or expressing racism. In some cases, the racial undertones are quite clear and quite problematic. In other cases, I argue that the mandate toward color-blind speech in our mainstream culture provides no other effective ways to discuss race. After all, the codes exist precisely because they work. This is all the more clear in my analysis of incoherence. Rather than argue that incoherence is always a crutch for racism or ignorance, as some prior studies have done, I demonstrate how incoherence can be a struggle to communicate. Specifically, it can be an attempt to reconcile color-blind discourse with a deep and strong need to talk about race.

Chapter 4 looks even deeper into this racial discourse, exploring the specific ways that diversity is discussed and valued within these communities. I argue that despite the glowingly positive talk around diversity, and the genuine desire to celebrate and see it maintained, active residents still unintentionally re-create a "white habitus" inside these racially diverse communities. That is, their race and diversity talk is still structured around a white norm, and their actions specifically but often unintentionally work to preserve advantages for whites, often to the detriment of people of color. Indeed, it is this white habitus which serves as the foundation of color-blind ideologies and the somewhat superficial diversity discourse that whites, as the majority of active residents, employ. This creates an unintended cycle of privilege rather than anything truly diverse and democratic.

Chapter 5 details the complex ways that these whites negotiate their racial identities in these communities. The setting of a diverse community is a fertile location for whites to become aware of and articulate their racial identities. Where much of whiteness studies in the past has remained ambivalent about whether it is even possible for whites to develop a racial self-awareness, I demonstrate that the specific contexts of crime, diversity, and political organizing in these communities are a catalyst for whites to discuss their racial identity. Indeed, their whiteness cannot be taken for granted in such settings; with that often comes cognizance of their racial privilege. I detail how some whites even code-switch in these settings; code switching is not only something under-privileged actors do for survival. Further, and perhaps most critically, I also examine the many ways that whites are indirectly negotiating their racial identities in these communities. Even when unstated, in these communities and in others, there are many forms of talk and action that are predicated on a white person's understanding of her own race. In the past, weariness to discuss one's whiteness explicitly has often been equated with a lack of racial awareness. Instead, I argue that there are many ways in which whites are often negotiating their white racial identity in everyday situations, which illuminates the complex dynamics of race and racism in ways previously unrecognized.

And finally, chapter 6 discusses the implications and opportunities arising from both the missteps and the successes detailed in this book. It is here that I provide data on the strong mismatch between the communities themselves and the income levels and racial demographics of the schools. This is one of several important blind spots in community efforts to date, one that if targeted through community efforts and investments could go a long way toward maintaining the diversity of these communities. Much of chapter 6 is devoted to changes at the national and community levels that could intentionally, rather than circumstantially, sustain these communities in the future. Only then will they move from being strong examples of noble efforts to truly exemplary models for the nation.

3

COLOR-BLIND IDEOLOGIES IN A LIBERAL, DIVERSE COMMUNITY

The focus of this chapter is how the national thinking about race, specifically that of color-blindness, impacts communities that are directly handling issues of race. In particular, given that the identities of these communities are specifically racially diverse, residents who are active inside these communities must navigate a simultaneous race cognizance and, as this chapter reveals, a complicity with the color-blind ideologies and discourse so prevalent in the nation. Sometimes this means using the frames of color-blindness directly, turning a blind eye, at least in their discussion, to the matters of race that are structuring a situation in their community. When this is difficult to manage, residents rely on coded racial talk to express the racial elements of a situation while still refusing direct discussion of race. Finally, when this is most challenging, residents have trouble discussing matters at all. They become nearly incoherent in their discussion of the role of race in their communities and in their lives. Yet rather than dismiss these codes or incoherence as intentionally covertly racist or simply incomprehensible, as some scholars have done in the past, I highlight the deep-seated struggle that these residents are facing not just in their discussion of race, but more importantly, in the ways that they try to work with racial issues in their communities.

NATIONAL THINKING ABOUT RACE

As discussed in the introduction to this book, color-blindness has, at least for the past several decades, dominated national thinking and discussion about race in the United States. The basic premise of color-blind ideology is that the problems of racism and segregation made so vivid during the Civil Rights Movement have been solved; all that is left is individual motivation and overcoming cultural barriers to achieve the American Dream. This ideological system is quite logical in that regard, given that the series of legal victories secured in the 1950s and 1960s do prohibit formal segregation in housing, schools, etc. It is for this reason that Eduardo Bonilla-Silva (2003) calls this framework "abstract liberalism"—the principles of equal opportunity that would create individual achievement are present in our laws and value systems. Further, affirmative action and other efforts toward multiculturalism in the past several decades have likely contributed to the impression that we have done enough as a nation, some say too much, to overcome the racism in our past.

What this thinking typically misses is the continued significance of that past in shaping the present. For example, while redlining was formally abolished in 1968 as a formal and legal strategy for mandating segregation in housing, the accumulated wealth from generations of racial privilege for whites have contributed to continued inequality. Given that wealth transfers primarily through inheritance in the United States, and the fact that most Americans hold their wealth in their home equity, race is still a driver in the constitutions of neighborhoods today. Those neighborhoods impact access to quality education, social networks, job opportunities, health care, decent food, and a host of other measures that reproduce racial inequalities.

Racial stereotypes, which were created to legitimate those formal systems of racism from slavery to Jim Crow, have also not abated in the post-Civil Rights era. Many whites and a smaller but significant number of people of color continue to believe that culture is what reproduces these inequalities, despite there being no clear evidence that this is the case. The same lack of evidence, or the existence of counterevidence, holds little sway in commonly held perceptions of crime, fertility rates, welfare usage, legal residence, terrorism, family values, and a host of other racialized issues. These ideas help "explain" racial matters for many Americans, especially when connected to the major frames of color-blind racism.

Color-blind ideology's major frames, or "set paths for interpreting information," were identified in 2003 by Eduardo Bonilla-Silva. His book, *Racism without Racists: Color-Blind Racism and the Persistence of Racial Inequality in the United States*, has shaped the sociological examination of racial inequalities. The frames, discussed below, are related to one another in that they support the general argument that continued racial inequalities can be explained by "anything but race," and more specifically, anything but racism. This includes any significant accumulation of past advantages for whites, and any forms of continued racism, privilege, or discrimination today. It is specifically that insistence on the exclusion of racism as a variable that makes these explanations ideological. They specifically take plausible and empirically defendable racism-related explanations for racial inequality off the table, and insist that they do not matter. It thus obscures our view of reality.

The first major frame of color-blind racism, as discussed briefly above, is abstract liberalism. Abstract liberalism emphasizes individual choice, "using ideas associated with political liberalism . . . and economic liberalism . . . in an *abstract* manner to explain racial matters" (Bonilla-Silva 2003, 28). This is in essence the idea of meritocracy, or a restatement of the ethic of the American Dream. The second is naturalization, which similarly explains things like segregation, be it in neighborhoods, schools, or friendship circles, as *only* a matter of personal choice or preference. This familiar frame argues that it is "only natural" that "birds of a feather flock together," or that "like attracts like." Because this is an inherently ahistorical and depoliticized stance, it also sees no harm in these continuing forms of segregation. After all, if the segregation is voluntary, who can complain? The third frame is cultural racism, which argues that any patterns of inequality stem from cultural values and norms rather than from any forces of racism or discrimination. This can take a positive form, as in the Model Minority stereotype which praises Asians for their "values"; a neutral form, which leaves unexamined the assumed traits of privileged groups like whites; or a negative form, as in the culture of poverty myth that has historically been and continues to be applied to people of color, including Asians until the Cold War. The final frame is the minimization of racism. While all of the frames minimize racism, this frame does so explicitly through common refrains like "the past is the past," "I didn't own any slaves," "I'm not a racist," the allegation that groups challenging racism are "playing the race card," etc.

As Bonilla-Silva and Forman note, "Uncovering ideology involves finding common *interpretive repertoires*, story lines or argumentation schemata" (2000, 52) which help the speaker navigate their world in ways that make a specific kind of sense. The four frames of color-blind racism do exactly that. However, that world may or may not fit neatly into the schema that discourse provides. There may be certain features that don't fit, or a frame that doesn't fully work, especially when we examine their use in real-world environments. As Van den Berg emphasizes, "The dilemmatic nature of discourse isn't a pre-given characteristic of assumed belief systems. Rather, it is accomplished in the concrete circumstances of social interaction" (2003, 136). To date, most studies that explore the use of color-blind ideologies have asked people to describe their views in universal or hypothetical settings. In this book, I explore how they are deployed in a concrete social setting. Exploring how active residents of diverse communities make sense of their communities and their associated issues relative to this color-blind racial discourse demonstrates the strength of this ideology, and the difficulty that even people in liberal, racially diverse communities find in talking and thinking outside of it.

LIBERAL FORMS OF COLOR-BLINDNESS IN COMMUNITY TALK

Bonilla-Silva's work, which used survey data from adults in the Detroit metropolitan area and in-depth interviews with college students in three regions, as well as much of the work that has followed, have left little doubt as to the prevalence of color-blind frames around the nation. In short, we know the four common frames of the color-blind ideology, and we know that this ideology and these frames are strongly shared throughout mainstream America. Once we come to recognize them, we hear them repeatedly on television, from politicians, in our families, and in our schools. Yet despite this recognition, we have fewer concrete, local studies that examine how they play out in specific rather than abstracted terms. That is, rather than asking people in general how they view common policies like welfare or affirmative action to identify the frames, we need to begin to examine how these ideologies and discourse, or ways of speaking, impact real-life, local settings. As Jason Rodriquez notes, "Racial ideology is experienced in distinct locations, even as it is shaped by discourses circulating at a national level and spiraling out of a racialized social system. Specifying the distinctly local manifestations of the dominant racial ideology extends our knowledge of how ideology operates in the everyday lives of individuals" (2006, 663). This is critical in a book like this, where I examine how the good intentions of committed, liberal people in diverse neighborhoods may falter when faced with concrete community action. That is, this way of thinking about race has very real consequences for the decisions, actions, and inactions taken in these communities.

Residents in these communities, despite being mostly liberal and, as the next chapter will show, pro-diversity, still made frequent use of the frames of color-blind racism. In fact, they did so in a way that is complicit with liberal frameworks, yet still upholds the larger framework of color-blindness. Far from being an ideology that only resonates with conservatives or bigots, it is something that has also influenced those working to support liberal policies and initiatives in the United States. Examining the use of color-blind ideologies among racially diverse communities' most active residents has powerful implications for the community itself. After all, these are the people, after the elected officials, who have the most power over the policy and development decisions in these communities. If they use color-blind ideologies, even in liberal-seeming ways, they are running the risk of being unable to handle the very real significance of race in their communities, as later sections in this chapter also show. As a result, as this book demonstrates, they ultimately practice a deep ambivalence about race and diversity in thought, talk, and community action. This ambivalence, through its unintentional recreation of white privilege and, as I demonstrate in chapter 4, a white habitus, could easily undermine the very diversity that, in principle and in their genuine discussions, they say they wish to defend.

Abstract Liberalism

Abstract liberalism is arguably the dominant frame of a color-blind ideology, as this frame mandates a belief that we have already achieved equal opportunity, and evaluates individual achievement on those grounds. This frame is directly meritocratic, seeing individual drive as the only factor shaping success. As such, it echoes the dominant ideology of the American Dream: "You can make it if you try; pull yourself up by your bootstraps." It is for that reason notable that abstract liberalism was never used directly by the mostly-liberal residents in my study. All offered something other than rugged individualism, which certainly has a conservative flair, as an explanation for racial outcomes. Instead, most discussed context or specific social structures, often to sympathize with the racial groups under discussion.

In the following passage, Todd had been discussing a spike of crime in Rogers Park that he said was coupled with an increase in development around the year 2000:

> You push around enough people of little means, little education, and, you know, things start to explode. You know, there's a gang component to that, but there's also just simply a sociological component to that, where, "Oh," you know, "You've lived here your whole life. You're an 18 year-old kid of little means, probably third, fourth generation living in poverty". . . . You know, I witnessed a lot more aggression on the street. . . . But on the flip side of all that, I'm not as struck by that as a lot of people as being odd or uncommon. I sort of *understand*. I'm not saying it's right. But I understand it.

Todd had been speaking specifically about times when he was harassed by black teens, in his estimation, because he is a white adult. Rather than becoming defensive, he discussed potential causes, perhaps cultural or structural, while still retaining a focus on race. He emphasized his belief that he understands, and indeed sympathizes with, such aggression—even if he makes a number of perhaps problematic assumptions in doing so.

This sympathetic talk about structures was common among almost all of the people I interviewed, who worked to acknowledge the realities of crime in their communities without making too-easy categorizations of who the criminals are and why they are engaging in crime. When I asked Shannon about the challenges in her community, Rogers Park, she said:

> We have a high incidence of drug and gang activity. High incidence of breaking into the cars by the el tracks. I live close to [an el] stop, which is where they just installed the blue light. So that's a huge discussion about how it affects crime or not. How it affects the overall feeling of the community.
>
> For me, one of my personal opinions about all of this that a lot of the people who are involved in any of the activity are younger, in our neighborhood at least. There definitely are older—I know that when I was going to buy in the neighborhood I did look how many sex offenders there were and there were quite a few living in the neighborhood. And they're older guys who've been convicted. So there's a lot of criminals in the neighborhood that are older, but the one—the thing I always focus on—the, the ones that I hear more about, and that's usually been young adults or young kids who are out on the street with nothing better to do. And that's a problem that we have across the United States, not just in Rogers Park.

In the above passage, Shannon discussed potential reasons why young people may participate in criminal activity, not only in Rogers Park but also across the nation. She devoted equal consideration to the crimes in her community that are not typically coded as young and black. Further, after she made this statement, she lamented her own inability to contribute to after-school programs to solve the "nothing better to do" problem she had theorized. Doing so meant that she further took ownership in the issue, rather than placing individual or cultural blame on the perpetrators.

A similar strategy was used by another Rogers Park resident, Mitch, who had also been speaking about teens having "something better to do" in the community:

> Well [my] attitude is—the people aren't the problem. It's the circumstances they're put in are the problem. So if we improve people's lives and give them productive things to do and constructive ways to engage in the community, then they'll participate in the community in more positive ways and everybody will benefit. Obviously we don't want poverty; if we could lift people out of poverty that's the ultimate goal, but you don't want

people that are living in poverty to have to suffer, so you wanna improve their lives any way you can.

And that's what we're trying to do. Especially, you know, the American ideal is that anyone born in any circumstances can rise above it, and the way you can ensure that is by giving kids a good education and positive influences in their lives, and there's no reason that you should condemn a kid to a lifetime of poverty just because he was born in poverty. So give them any type of chance to get out of it, you've got to give them a good education, and education extends beyond just the classroom, so that's what we're hoping [our organization] will do.

In that part of our discussion, Mitch directly critiqued the foundations of abstract liberalism, especially in his statement that "people aren't the problem." In so doing, he explores poverty, education, and civic engagement as both problems and potential solutions to lessen the impact of continued inequalities in his community.

The absence of abstract liberalism in my interview data suggests a partial departure from color-blind frames in diverse, liberal communities. Instead, participants emphasized circumstances or social structures, most often social class, when explaining the racial inequalities in their communities. This is something, remember, that I never directly asked them to do. This makes their refusal of this particular discursive frame all the more significant. Others invoked a psychological explanation. Eric, a resident of Edgewater, had been discussing an area of the community that he had identified as a problem and explained its dynamics as follows:

The sergeant or whoever's the top cop said that there's one of the highest concentrations of people living in that area because of all the multi-unit buildings in the city. Which, you know, like, Cabrini-Green, I think at its heyday, there were, like, a million people living in a one-mile radius, on top of each other, which created horrible, horrible results. Because it was just too densely populated, you know, I mean, people were literally living on top of each other, so it just opens up crime and trash and blight and . . . I mean, people can't think in that close proximity to each other. So that's one thing that—that's why that section of the neighborhood gets a lot of press, you know, the historic perspective, bad press for crime, gangs, drugs, because it's such a high concentration of human beings.

As discussed in chapter 2, the issue of density is a common concern for residents, and the failure of public housing sites like Cabrini-Green were commonly referenced examples. However, it is significant that Eric emphasized an inability to *think* in that context, linking Cabrini-Green and all it has come to represent with regard to race, crime, and poverty in the American imagination with a section of Edgewater that many residents identify as a problem. In so doing, Eric simultaneously coded that area as a problem and sought a racially-neutral, psychological explanation for that problem. He refused abstract liberalism and cultural racism in his account of the situation, but did so in a deeply racialized context, the nuances of which I explore later in this chapter. Perhaps for this reason, Eric's passage best represents how active residents negotiate the frame of abstract liberalism in these communities.

While abstract liberalism was not directly articulated among active residents in the neighborhoods I studied, their refusal of this frame may still affirm color-blind ideologies. Richard Schaefer has argued that "educated people learn acceptable responses that can be employed especially in the context of questionnaires and interviews by social scientists" (1996, 5). Following Schaefer, George Yancey, in his study of racially integrated communities, notes that while education is empirically linked to support for integration, those with higher education may not harbor less prejudice, but rather learn to produce acceptable responses (1999, 280). Maria Krysan has also shown how those with higher educational levels tend to express their ambivalence about integration through structural and social explanations, which are still fundamentally racialized, rather than by use of overt stereotyping of minority communities (2002, 693).

While never blaming individuals through the abstract liberalism frame, residents in Rogers Park, Edgewater, and Uptown made use of all of the other three major frames of color-blind ideology, traces of which are present in the excerpts above and others that will be explored below. This simultaneous refusal and compliance with color-blind frames points to the deeply-seated hegemony of the ideology, for even active members of a stably diverse neighborhood, who care about issues of race and inequality in their communities and who appreciate the diversity in their neighborhood, cannot escape its influence. Their refusal of abstract liberalism as a dominant frame of color-blind racism indicate liberal views around race and inequality, but their break from color-blind ideologies is rarely complete.

Cultural Racism

This is perhaps most vivid when participants make use of what has been called the "cultural racism" frame of color-blind ideologies. This frame makes use of the widespread belief in cultural differences among racial groups, particularly as a determining factor in continued inequalities. It uses the idea of culture to explain common stereotypes such as why "Asians are so good at math," "Black people are so likely to abuse welfare," and "Whites are the moral citizen" in modern America. While I often explain this frame to my students as the one that can sound the most traditionally racist for its categorical descriptions of any race's imagined "culture," even Bonilla-Silva notes how this frame can also be used in apologetic, sympathetic, and, of course, problematic ways. It is in these apologetic or sympathetic forms that this frame demonstrates the uniquely liberal flavor of color-blind ideology in these diverse communities.

Without exception, this frame was used in the sympathetic rather than accusatory form that Bonilla-Silva also identifies in his national study. Here Patty, of Rogers Park, uses the frame in a story she was telling me about her perceptions of Chicago's public schools:

> One thing, and I hope this doesn't sound racist, it's not meant to be: One thing you *never* hear, is the schools that are struggling so much, I know a lot of the teachers in those schools, and they are giving their all to their job.
>
> But there are students coming that are not . . . first of all there's all kinds of nonsense goes on at home. They don't have proper meals, there might be, god knows what they do all night, the kids fall asleep in class. The news was on the other night about closing those schools and making them small schools. A freshman student from [a local public school] was interviewed, and he was black. And they said, "Well what do you think the problem is?" And this little boy said, in terms of the students that weren't doing well, he said, "*It's because they families don't care.*"
>
> But you can't say that. And you never see it and you never hear it. *He* said it. But he was a student and he was black. And he could say it. But

nobody else could say it . . . I know what some of this stuff is that happens, but nobody says it, but he said *"They families don't care."* And that's—that's really what it's all about. . . . So it's very sad.

Note how in this story Patty repeatedly emphasized the poor grammar of this young black man on the news. She also bemoaned how she is unable to critique what she *imagines* to be true about home environments of black public school students in Chicago, because she is white and could be perceived as racist. Her cultural explanations, while relying heavily on racial stereotypes about black families, are sympathetic, as evidenced in her statement that "it's very sad" and her celebration of the teachers' efforts.

Her explanation differs significantly from Anthony, of Edgewater, in his mostly racially conscious explanation for struggling public schools in Chicago:

So the people who can afford to send their kids to private schools or have the savvy or clout to send them to some magnet school will do that, and those that don't go to the noncompetitive local schools.

And then their kids don't—and it really strikes a sore note for me, because most of those kids are black. And it's not a black-white thing, it's more of a class issue. But still, most of those kids are African American, and they have for years—maybe it's getting better—not received a competitive education, generation after generation after generation after generation. [Even] the housing. So those issues really ring, I mean, it's just kind of all there.

While Anthony's assessment of the schools is more race cognizant than Patty's, it still de-emphasizes race in favor of class, a common theme in the minimization of racism frame explored below. He alternates between a focus on race as it relates to opportunity and a class-*not-race* explanation that is complicit with color-blind ideology.

This use of cultural racism among the liberals in this community is not usually as seething as the indictments of "black culture" often being imagined among respondents in national studies like Eduardo Bonilla-Silva's. In these communities, it is conciliatory, reluctant, but most often challenges assumptions connected to stereotype, rather than the stereotype itself. Todd, another Rogers Park resident, does this in his commentary on stereotypes about welfare abuse. We had been talking about how he responds to questions that he frequently gets about Rogers Park's safety, questions that he himself identified as racially loaded. He said:

> But, you know, there's other issues. Relatively speaking compared to lots of places, yeah, those stereotypes are true. With that diversity and inclusion, and people who are working within the system, whether it's Section 8 or other things, you'll find a lot higher concentration of people that have lived on the fringe, whether it's because of, you know, their mental capacity, or their race or their—how they grew up in terms of economics. But the reality is we've been an open-armed community for a long, long time. And that's created a fair number of problems as well.

Here it is clear how the adoption of cultural racism takes on a particular liberal, sympathetic, and even structural flavor in this liberal diverse community, as Todd is both conceding what he feels to be the fact of a stereotype about crime and welfare abuse among racial minorities, which upholds color-blind racism. Yet he does so while linking the, in his mind, true, stereotype to something other than the failure of individual drives.

This sympathetic flavor within cultural racism was not absent in Bonilla-Silva's national study, but in the context of these communities, it almost always invoked an educated-seeming stance, as evidenced by Margaret, an Uptown resident, who was speaking about the challenge of involving some of Uptown's Asian community in its leadership structures: "And leadership, I don't think emerges in the Asian communities like it emerges in our communities and in some other various nationalities." She said this as though this common and harmful stereotype about Asians was simply a fact, thereby excluding the possibilities of racism, marginalization, distrust, or other political factors shaping Asian political leadership, or lack thereof, in Uptown. This is similar to Richard Schaefer's analysis of racism among educated whites. He argues that even when educated whites attribute factors of social life to institutional structures, "in effect we have a more cultured, more sanitized 'blaming the victim'" (1996, 6).

Some residents sidestepped a direct use of cultural racism in broad-sweeping terms by making distinctions within racial communities. Here Evelyn had been discussing Edgewater's successes in recent years, but added:

I mean, [we] still have a way to go on Winthrop and Kenmore. And here's the issue, you know, that you get into racial and I think that the problem of—of, um, Kenmore and Winthrop is partially racial, but racial in the sense that the hooligans and the bad people have made an impact in the area. And there are plenty of non-whites that are very good citizens and want a safe, clean place to live just like everybody else. Um, but—but somehow or another with the four-plus-ones you got the, uh, uh, wrong element of the black community in there.

Evelyn spoke with uncertainty and hesitation at this moment in our discussion, whereas in most of our discussion she spoke with ease and confidence. This may be due to her reliance on some racial codes around the four-plus-ones, which I discuss later in this chapter. However, she was not alone in expressing the "plenty of good people" sentiment with regard to black populations in these communities. Several others also did so, and often made the same move as Evelyn in asserting the cultural explanations for a *segment* of the black community rather than the community as a whole. Rhetorically, this may distance her from outright, overt racism, but it still involves the same racial stereotypes that are typically applied to all.

That is not to say that the "traditional" form of the cultural racism frame never emerged. Kurt, of Uptown, had been discussing feeling unsafe in certain areas near where he lives, and said:

I had lunch today with one of my best friends from college, and he is a man of color who was reared by aristocratic southern black people, aunts and grandparents. And what's always been stunning about knowing this young man is that he is not one who is very big on his own race. Some people tend to use the phrase, well, they're ghetto or they behave black.

Well, this kid doesn't behave in this manner at all. He loathes that. He doesn't understand why people can't work beyond the stereotype that they have brought on themselves. We've had very limited discussion of this area because he doesn't dwell on it. His opinion is he's just another person and, well, the best way to characterize him is what he once said to me about the way he views the world, and that is that he makes no apologies for having read as a child.

Kurt relied on his black friend from college, whom he refers to as a "kid," to make assertions about the truth behind stereotypes about black values and culture. He holds up his friend as an exception to an otherwise-confirmed rule. Further, he does so as one possible way of justifying his fear of black-on-white crime in Uptown. In his case, despite the "confirmation" of this racial stereotype, the story is still strategic and "studied" rather than overt in its racism, which still gives it a distinct, perhaps liberal, flair.

The cultural racism frames invoked by active residents of these racially diverse, liberal communities take quite a different form than in national studies like Bonilla-Silva's, where discourse was tied to universal or hypothetical contexts rather than to actual and situated ones. While the cultural explanations are deeply problematic for their relationship to racial or ethnic stereotypes, it is significant that the form that these explanations took were almost always not only sympathetic and well-intentioned, but also seemingly "educated"—whether informed by fact or not.

The goal is not to decide whether or not the people I've quoted in this section, or in this book, are racist. In fact, most seemingly were not. Further, there is little scholarly or practical utility in determining who is racist or who is not, or in discovering exactly what racism looks and sounds like (see Trepagnier 2006). Such practices deflect attention from the processes and complexities of a racialized social system. Drawing on Joe Feagin's work, I often remind my students that we are all [hopefully] recovering racists because we all live in a society that accumulates privileges and disadvantages around race. My point, instead, is to notice the complex terrain residents of these communities are navigating, simultaneously "informed" by cultural racism so easily adopted from popular culture, and working hard to forge community in a diverse environment. Here if nowhere else are the constraints of color-blind ideologies, and the vast system of misinformation that perpetuates it, most apparent.

Naturalization

Another frame of color-blind ideology is called naturalization, which explains continued racial segregation (in schools, neighborhoods, relationships) in nonracial terms. This frame allows *only* for personal preference and naturalized ideas about social groups to "explain" low levels of interracial contact in neighborhoods, institutions, and in our daily lives. While the reality is that personal choice, networks, social class, race, and other factors are all part of the complex mix that explains continued segregation in the United States, the naturalization frame specifically de-emphasizes race as a factor. Instead, it favors explanations of social class, a hallmark of the minimization of racism frame, or "natural human tendencies," both of which fare well with the particular liberal character of color-blind ideologies found pervasively in these communities.

Residents in these communities often discussed "segments" of the communities, indicating that residents are aware of the segregation within these diverse neighborhoods. In Uptown, as discussed in chapter 2, residents typically discussed community on a block-by-block basis. In Edgewater, residents discussed three distinct areas: Andersonville, which is often perceived as separate from Edgewater altogether; the Winthrop-Kenmore corridor, which is often recognized for its past history of crime and continued concentration of rental housing; and the area west of Broadway, where most people I interviewed lived, an area dominated by single-family homes and attractive three-flat condos. Rogers Park was spoken about by its quadrants, and there seemed to be community consensus that the "real" Rogers Park was its southeastern segment, with Devon Avenue, West Rogers Park, and the area north of Howard being somewhat separate communities.

The reality of a segmentation or segregation within these communities is not at issue here. It is the explanation for this segregation that the active residents supply that will most strongly relate to their community activity. After all, if they don't think racial segregation is an issue, they won't tackle it as a problem. Todd, of Rogers Park, explained this segregation as follows:

> People tend to still segregate *themselves* by race, I think. More than they would like to think. . . . That happens because, you know, just how Chinatown becomes Chinatown. People tend to congregate with like people. . . . This building becomes an African American building because, you know, an African American may own it, and it's just, "Hey, I got this friend," "OK, sure." "They're—yeah, they got a job, they don't owe this that and the other thing, their credit's OK, move in!" and these things just sort of happen.

Todd's temptation to naturalize what is in fact social behavior is a benchmark of the naturalization frame. While this explanation does reference the reality of social networks, it also erases the significance of such networks for surviving racism and discrimination, which is the often-untold story of the creation of urban cultural or immigrant communities.

Like all four frames of color-blind ideology, talk about segregation also minimized race as a determining factor in current housing and other public spaces. Walter, an Uptown resident, noted, "And that's the one sad thing. We have essentially segregation in the school, and—and it's more economic on that. And, uh, so you have a lot of people abandoning the city, go out in the suburbs." Walter fuses issues of social class, typically a hallmark of the minimization of racism frame discussed below, with naturalization. This is again a way in which color-blindness takes on a particular flavor within these liberal, diverse communities. The style or larger argument being made among liberals and/or those in diverse neighborhoods may differ from color-blind discourses, but the logic remains the same: continued structural racism and the significance of race is specifically ruled out as a potential cause or condition for the social landscape. Again, as I argue in chapter 6, when it's off the table for analysis, it's off the table for intentional action.

Minimization of Racism

This is perhaps nowhere more vivid than in the minimization of racism frame. While all frames of color-blind racism work to minimize racism in some way, this frame does so directly, arguing that racism is either an element of America's past or has been greatly improved to the point of virtual negligibility. In Bonilla-Silva's study there were a variety of strategies used to minimize racism; in these communities the most common was to emphasize class over race. This rhetorical move does not typically allow for considerations of class and race, but rather of class instead of race. This specific exclusion of race is what makes the frame ideological and helps the speaker uphold a color-blind narrative. Much like the naturalization frame above, the function of this frame is to exclude or strongly diminish race and racism from an otherwise reasonable list of reasons why neighborhoods may be segregated. So while social class is certainly a critically important element shaping social and racial inequalities, an emphasis on "class *not* race" takes on an ideological significance.

The strategy of discussing social class inequality also helps uphold the distinct liberal flavor of color-blind racism in these communities. This is perhaps best exemplified by the following passage from Wendy, a Rogers Park resident who spoke in other places during our interview about her hope that Rogers Park would remain a racially diverse community into the future:

> *Wendy:* I always made a vow to myself I would want to live in a mixed community, you know. And ultimately coming to Uptown and to Edgewater, this was the epitome of what I had been looking for. It really was.
>
> *MAB:* Do you worry about these neighborhoods losing this character over time?
>
> *Wendy:* At times I do. At times I do because of economics more than anything else. Economics. Whether people can afford to stay here or not.

While Wendy was speaking about the very real threat of increased development pricing working-class minorities out of the community, her emphasis on this being "economics more than anything else" is significant. Her concern is racial diversity, but she insists that the dynamics driving this are nonracial. While gentrification certainly happens on economic fronts, its racial components are well-established (Shaw & Sullivan 2007; Smith 1998; Martinez-Cosio 2007; Nyden, Edlynn, & Davis 2006). Wendy seems to know this, given her concerns. As such, her choice to emphasize economics explicitly over race reveals the pressure toward color-blind ideologies even in these liberal, diverse communities.

Recall that I never asked residents to explain the neighborhood's diversity to me, nor to rank factors shaping diversity in terms of their importance. This makes the frequency at which people did so all the more revealing. Todd even celebrated Barack Obama's presidential campaign for affirming his assessment of the significance of class over race:

> I'm glad to see—and it's Barack who's finally started bringing up this issue in the presidential campaign now, is, you know, by and large it's become a class issue. And maybe that's been an issue longer in the history of this

country than anybody ever wanted to admit and that the race issue wasn't necessarily as big a problem as it was a class issue.

What this discourse misses, of course, is an appreciation for the ways that race and class are so closely knit together in the United States, both historically and today. While a class analysis is still more liberal, critical of U.S. institutions, and as such not as power-blind as many of the rest of the frames of color-blind ideology, it still quite willfully evades the social and political consequences of a racialized social system. Maria Krysan, in her study of white racial attitudes around integration, has noted "it was easy for . . . respondents who gave [a class-based] answer to distance themselves from holding negative racial attitudes because the forces of economics and the ways 'society' should be blamed" (2002, 693). This strategy is especially significant for whites, who collectively benefit from a race-evasive analysis in their everyday lives (Hill 2008). It moves responsibility from a personal to a distant source, retains a "liberal" perspective, and still upholds a color-blind ideology.

While the "class not race" finding was most common, there were other strategies to minimize racism used among participants in this study. Patty, of Rogers Park, had been speaking about racial tensions in Chicago's public schools, and remarked:

> *Patty:* Fortunately, there isn't as much, I don't see as much of that now. I think race is not the issue that it was before. You know, I don't know. I mean, it was more of an issue—what are we talking about? The '70s? The, 20, 30 years ago? It was more of an issue then. For, I'm not talking about for me. It was never a big deal for us. Um, but for the people that it was a big deal for, it doesn't seem to be as big a deal for anymore.
>
> *MAB:* What do you mean by that?
>
> *Patty:* I'm, I'm not sure. (*laughter*)

She then quickly changed the subject. While certainly there has been much racial progress in the decades since the 1970s, asserting that race is not the issue that it was before, either broadly or in relation to local schools, is a common refrain in the minimization of racism frame. Later in the conversation she spoke of this sentiment directly in relation to Rogers Park.

And I always felt that one reason Rogers Park could manage so well, [with] diversity, is there's a mentality here that can look past things like color and language, to the person, you know, and I think there's a lot of that. And I think that's why Rogers Park can hold the way it does.

While many residents discussed a mentality, or a certain type of person, being the glue for their diverse community, the concurrent minimization of racism embodied in "looking past things like color and language, to the person" does not allow for a serious examination of race in the community.

As Anthony, of Edgewater, notes below:

I felt residents, if you said there was a problem here, you were automatically attacked as a gentrifier and anti-poor, when there were legitimate concerns of safety and systemic policy issues that kept things progressing. If you have 13 homeless shelters, why are you adding another one? Why are you saying, if a certain census tract has up to 40 percent of the population already subsidized, why are you adding more subsidized housing there?

And that was shot down with anti-poor, you're just a gentrifier, blah-blah-blah. And we said, well, by HUD's own standards, it's too high. Why are you putting more? Why not fix up the existing affordable housing that you have and then provide more home ownership, whether it be affordable home ownership or market rate? That was our position, or my position.

As concerns like Anthony's demonstrate, and the next chapter explores in more detail, these color-blind ideologies can also hinder that diversity from being maintained. Sol Tax, in documenting the efforts of Hyde Park to become integrated rather than re-segregated in the 1950s, noted: "nothing at all could have been done if racial integration had not been an explicit and integral part of the plan . . . nothing would have happened without deliberate social action" (1959, 22). Color-blind ideologies do not allow for this deliberate action. They persuade us that they cannot even be discussed.

Denise, an Edgewater resident, similarly defined her neighborhood's identity as quite emphatically color-blind:

Denise: I mean, we are really color blind. We are, you know, there just— there isn't the . . . you don't hear about the hatred and the unfortunate remarks that are made elsewhere because it's a family here. It's a family here.

MAB: And why do you think that is?

Denise: Because we're—we tolerate. We tolerate. Our differences are acute, but we tolerate each other. And it doesn't matter to us that you're a gay man or a black woman. It doesn't matter to us. You're a person. And that's who you have living here.

This claim is despite other places in our interview where she discussed efforts she was undertaking to increase police monitoring of black male teenagers, whom she referred to as "hooligans." However, it's important to note that Denise does seem to mean what she says about tolerance in her community. However, she draws very clear and specific lines around "her" community, explaining that the teens "are not our kids." In so doing, she draws a strong symbolic boundary around the problem area in the neighborhood she's referencing. Others, like Adam, dismissed the possibility of racism in contexts like this outright: "It's the perception. I mean, it all comes down—and I don't—I really don't think it's racism. I think it's . . . it's the idea of people hanging out on the streets, and it's the despair that's just so in your face at times in Uptown that frightens people." Yet the language around "people hanging out on the streets" and "despair" has long been racialized, as I explore more fully in my analysis of coded language that follows.

Refusing the Frames

Before analyzing that coded language, however, it is important to note that there were several participants, both white and people of color, in this study who never made use of color-blind ideologies in their conversation about race and diversity. These participants clustered around two categories—black men and progressive white men. While my sample is not broad enough to analyze these trends more broadly, they do have a relationship to other studies of color-blind ideologies and racial identity. For the black men in this study, who were very few in number (as African Americans were only 7 out of the 41 participants in this study), honest discussion of racial matters, including at times their own harassment by police or other community members, precluded a willingness to minimize the significance of race, and of racism more broadly. Given the small number of black men who are active in these communities, and the closely networked natures of these communities, I am choosing not to reveal their stories of harassment or negative interactions with whites for fear of compromising their anonymity. The Asian and Latino men, and women of color, either adhered to color-blind discourses or did not discuss stories like these (see O'Brien 2008).

The other group who refused color-blind ideologies were progressive white men. In chapter 5, I examine some of the ways that, given a refusal of these color-blind frames, they were able to speak honestly and reflect critically on their white identity in these diverse communities. In particular, this finding parallels Paul Croll's (2007) conception of white identity being most pronounced at either end of the political spectrum. The fact that women of all races adhered to the frames of color-blind racism is notable, as it also departs from Bonilla-Silva's finding that working-class white women are the most likely to be racial progressives and refuse color-blind ideologies. The interaction of race, gender, and social class is an ongoing site of research in this new area of situated, localized racial discourses. While this book offers some cursory findings in this regard, it more urgently suggests that much more research needs to be done to better understand the complex racial, gendered, class, and other dynamics which compel some to adhere to color-blind frames or gives the confidence and competence to others to break them.

CODED TALK

The section above demonstrated how even the liberal, pro-diversity residents of racially diverse communities have difficulty maneuvering outside of the frames of color-blind racism. This section explores their attempts to do so, particularly through reliance on racial codes. Racial codes are meant to communicate something about race without doing so directly, usually by making reference to familiar settings or characters. For example, phrases like "gang banger" and "Section 8 Housing" racialize a discussion without specifically naming any particular racial group. In this section I unpack these meanings and their relation to concrete community action. This dynamic is critical to understand, as it is the mostly white, liberal, pro-diversity residents in this study that are shaping local efforts around development, crime, beautification, and other community issues. They demonstrate not only the perils of well-meaning diversity efforts in the post-Civil Rights era, but also the link between common racial discourse and concrete social outcomes.

After cracking these codes and analyzing how and when they are used, I explore the role of incoherence, critical evidence that even well-intentioned people doing positive community work in diverse communities can still be so deeply inhibited by color-blind ideologies that they literally cannot speak. Studying racial codes and incoherence is a delicate process. It involves analyzing what people are *trying* to say, at times when they are specifically not saying it. As Picca and Feagin have argued, "The use of code language provides a good method of routinely signaling . . . views or acts . . . but disguising those views or acts from their targets" (2007, 168). While I think they are right in that at times this disguise is deliberate, I argue that codes are also used when no other ways to speak about an issue seem possible. This tension is particularly strong for those who are not necessarily active in reproducing racism, but are instead trying to articulate a pro-diversity stance in a color-blind society. As Van den Berg notes, "The co-occurrence of racist statements and denials of racism in an interviewee's discourse isn't always a matter of the careful use of rhetorical devices on behalf of strategic goals. On the contrary, contradictions in interviewee's discourse may point to a 'real' or substantive dilemma, i.e., a dilemma that cannot be solved by rhetorical means" (2003, 135). This is in fact evidenced by the reality that, as I will demonstrate, when the coded talk doesn't work or is refused, speakers falter in their speaking. They become incoherent.

Scholars are increasingly aware that coded talk is a key form of race-focused discussion. By use of racial codes, people can communicate fluently about crime, blight, drug dealing, education, culture, and a myriad of other issues in deeply racialized terms without ever naming a racial group or an associated racial stereotype. As Steyn and Foster note in their study of "white talk" in South Africa, "Crime is part of the perceived threat to the white order and the decline that is expected to accompany the failure to uphold white norms find expression in images which communicate danger, disintegration, decay, corruption, disease, and perversion" (2008, 38). In the following passage Patty, of Rogers Park, had been describing an interaction she'd had the morning of our interview with two people who had just moved into her neighborhood from an all-white community. She was telling them that I was going to interview her about her involvement in a racially diverse neighborhood, and said:

> *Patty:* And now they've got a whole bunch of friends that they didn't have before. . . . And I'm sure, she said "Well . . ." they weren't bothered by it. . . . "We wouldn't be here if we were looking at things like that." And she's right. They wouldn't.
>
> *MAB:* If they were "looking at things like that," meaning . . . .
>
> *Patty:* Um . . . iffy, a lot of . . . a lot of blight not too far away from some, um, uh, Section 8 housing in the next block, uh, you know, we've, we all live with that. But it's ma- it's what makes it neighborhoody. (*laughs*)

Notice how Patty has difficulty discussing what she sees to be the problems of the neighborhood in direct terms, using instead the word "it" and "things like that." When I asked her to clarify, she named Section 8 housing and blight—two very commonly racialized topics in these communities. At the same time, she lays claim to those elements of the neighborhood, saying that's what makes it "neighborhoody," and emphasizes the "OK"-ness of it. At this point in our conversation we had not been discussing race or blight. Diversity as a topic of conversation communicated the link between race, blight, and Section 8 housing even if her specific language did not.

Part of my strategy to ensure that I was properly understanding the codes was to map the references between interviewees. Jane Hill notes: "Following Foucault, I assume that deep principles determine what components of the message are explicit, and what components are recovered through inference" (2008, 33). If the same principles, specifically a shared discursive framework, are active in a concrete, local community, then these same inferences will likely be repeated among participants. Further, through references to specific events, they will emerge alongside to other clues that help me ensure that I have understood their meaning. It was through this process that other residents affirmed my understanding of these racial codes. For example,

Matthew, of Rogers Park, confirmed my understanding of the code around Section 8 housing as follows:

> I remember I had this very significant . . . conversation with one of the neighbors who I just assumed was this, like, sort of progressive open minded person because she was really into gardening and was really this kind of earthy person. And she just was so antagonistic towards Section 8 families and low-income families. . . . And it was shocking to me. I couldn't even imagine that people like that existed in the neighborhood who are progressive people.

Matthew's verification of this code was particularly useful, in that it cracks this racial code and specifically decouples it from the otherwise progressive or liberal identity of the neighborhood. It cracked both the code and the veneer around diversity that, as the next chapter describes, so many in the community maintain.

Carla, of Edgewater, discussed community meetings where the sentiment Matthew discussed was also active:

> *Carla:* You don't have to be in a cul-de-sac environment to have a cul-de-sac mindset, you know? [*laughs.*] Okay? There's some mindsets over here that should be in Naperville.
>
> *MAB:* Can you think of an example for an issue like that?
>
> *Carla:* Just thinking that renters, just having the mindset that the renters don't care about the property, that they're going to bring property values down. You know, that kind of thing . . .
>
> But just that unfounded fear that if we build more high-rises or we build four plus ones, I mean, that was really—those were really big issues. And those did have renters in them. And those four plus ones, I mean, you just say the word four plus one and you know . . . it kind of becomes you don't need to say anything else.

Carla's assertion that discussing public housing carried strong racial undertones was echoed among several community members. Further, Carla specifically defines a code, where a specific housing style, the "four-plus-one," stands in for blight. As Carla notes, "you don't need to say anything else."

The use of this racial code was common among residents who shared otherwise specific stories of negative incidents in the neighborhood. In the following passage Adam, of Edgewater, had been discussing strategies used to fight crime in his block: "I mean, we sit on our porches at night . . . and if somebody would just loiter in the street, or they didn't look like they belonged in the neighborhood, and they were talking too loud—like, I remember one night some teenagers were cussing, using foul language, so I called the police. You know, it was just that just constant pounding." While I do not know the race of the loiterers, the teenagers, or the people who "didn't look like they belonged in the neighborhood," I do know from a prior moment in the conversation that there were no black residents on his block, and I also was able to infer from many conversations throughout the three neighborhoods that negative stories involving teenagers were often stories about *black* teenagers—who as this resident indicates are indeed being carefully monitored and often heavily policed in all three communities.

The above examples reveal negative codes in their commentary or in their uncritical adoption by community members. Yet the power of the codes, and the color-blind ideology that insists upon them, is perhaps best illustrated by residents who critiqued racism in their community. Jackie, of Rogers Park, had been speaking about a recent aldermanic election:

> And it turned out that there was this silent, angry white vote that had bought homes up in what we call the Juneway Jungle, which had gotten gentrified. And there's these big, beautiful homes up there that have always been there, but there's also a bunch of buildings that they warehoused a bunch of underserved Section 8 people into. And now it's like, oh, no, we want our neighborhood back. Well, you put people there in the first place in this situation, versus, like, dispersing in different places, and then you let the buildings go to shit.

Jackie is critical of the "angry white vote" and those gentrifiers who are opposed to public housing, while at the same time referring to a heavily working-class black section of this community as the jungle—a deeply racialized, loaded term that was very common among neighborhood residents. While many have said that this is simply what this area is called in the community, it is still noteworthy that Jackie, and many of the residents, continues to use this language. Jane Hill, in her work, analyzes a variety of codes and discourses that are used quite innocently, but which through both history and connotation are often offensive to people of color. She notes, "I have never found any evidence that [whites] are not completely sincere in these objections [to the charge that their discourse is racialized], and I believe that the racializing functions . . . are genuinely invisible to them" (2008, 42). While the racializing function may remain invisible, the utility of these codes, for speakers, is not. They are used precisely because they work.

Rick, of Rogers Park, also used the jungle code when speaking about the same geographical area discussed above. Rick and I had been discussing improvements he'd like to see in the community: "I'd like to see Sheridan Road improved. . . . Even just opening up north of Howard, and what I mean by that is there is no egress in or out of 'the Jungle' quote-unquote. And they need to open up, on either side of the cemetery, a thoroughfare there. So you can get in and out." While his "quote-unquote" may be referencing how others speak about that area of the community and in that process challenging the code, he is still making the choice to use this code with me. He is also someone who here and at another juncture discussed feeling unsafe in areas that have a high density of African Americans, further complicating his choice to use the code "Jungle" in the context above.

This "jungle" language was used in all three communities in this book, further demonstrating its racialized rather than geographic nature. Walter, of Uptown, used the phrase when discussing a concentration of public housing in his community:

> One of our issues here in this community [is] we have a lot of nursing homes and HUD buildings, and Section 8 buildings, which are all good and needed. The only problem is, because of Alderman Shiller, down in the 46th, she likes to attract them. We've got overconcentration. And that's the wrong thing. You would think we'd learned that lesson when we created Cabrini-Green. And you're not doing those people any favor. You're creating a-a-a jungle for them . . .

In this passage, Walter invokes racial codes through mention of Cabrini-Green, HUD, Section 8 Buildings, and again the "jungle" discourse,

amidst a series of "ums" and "uhs" that were not present in other places
in his speech. This indicates an uneasy navigation of the racial codes,
the dynamics of which are explored in detail in the next section. This
is despite the claim that for Walter the issue is explained specifically as
density and not race, a finding indeed backed by a number of studies (see
Popkin et al 2000; Mitchell 1971; for a critique of neighborhood v. racial
stereotyping see Patillo 2001). In Walter's statement, color-blindness is
standing in the way of concretely discussing problems that are very real
for his community, in perception if not in reality. It both structures his
mode of communication, through his reliance on its codes, and inhibits
his mode of communication by narrowing the scope of what can be said.

Some residents demonstrated their awareness of these codes as
problematic, and spoke around them in ambivalent ways. Laurie was
answering my question about where she'd lived prior to Rogers Park and
said, "I guess what would be considered kind of a bad part of Chicago,
or at least a heavily populated black part of Chicago. I don't necessarily
consider it a bad part of Chicago, but there is a high level of crime in
the area." In that statement Laurie clarified her beliefs about that part
of Chicago and her comfort with it, but acknowledged the racial codes
that would make "heavily populated black" a "bad" part of town. Indeed,
after this comment she went on to criticize some friends of hers who had
been too fearful to spend time with her in that area. Laurie was naming
the code and its false racial pretenses. In so doing, she also affirmed that
I had been able to correctly crack it.

While most people were using or critiquing coded talk in ways that
were racially tolerant or merely uneasy, among some residents the
negative undertones of the racial codes were quite clear. Denise, of
Edgewater, had been discussing a long history of conflict with black
teens in a nearby area, and the ways that her community had organized
to challenge them:

> It's that kind of a thing where the hooligans are going like this [middle
> finger] to us. And they're also in the [park by the school]. . . . And then
> I went to the beat meeting on it, and then I'm gonna go to another beat
> meeting on it and say, you know, they're—these hooligans—they're pelt-
> ing youngsters with stones. Let's increase your patrols for an indefinite
> period of time. And now it's getting warm, so . . .

While she does not name the race of the "hooligans" she is describing, the area she is discussing is heavily populated by black teenagers after school hours. Anthony, also of Edgewater, affirms how common Denise's perception is:

> The [local] high school kids, they're good kids. However, when they come in and out, the bad element hides and mixes in between with them. So from the little old lady perspective, oh, those bad [local] high school kids, and the [other] kids are angels. That's not necessarily true, but that's the perception.

Later in the conversation Denise emphasized that they "are not our kids"—meaning that they are not residents of her section of the neighborhood, which is populated primarily by white homeowners. Further, she is not alone in naming this as a trouble spot in the community—discussion about this block and the teenagers who populate it in the afternoon hours was common among Edgewater residents. I lived very near the area she is referencing and I was told repeatedly by participants in this study to be careful on that block, one that I walked for years without fear or any sort of incident.

Other residents, like Hank, of Uptown, were quite creative about their coding. Hank had been speaking about drugs and crime in his community.

> What we found out a few years ago was that—I call them the local entrepreneurs of the neighborhood, you know—the kids selling drugs and that. . . . And also you notice, at least I do, the young entrepreneurs rarely cross over to our side of [the street] to dispense their wares because I think they know there's people watching them all the time.

Hank was referencing a remarkably effective strategy he and his neighbors had created to coordinate walks in order to maintain a physical presence at most hours of the day and night. Even so, when he spoke to me about "local entrepreneurs" and their "dispensing" of "their wares," his eyes twinkled and he smirked, a physical signal to me that he was proud of his code and its success. Scholars have noted the creativity present in many racial codes (Picca & Feagin 2007), and Hank's code is a key example. Here he resists the more common code "gang bangers"

for a more politically correct, more heavily coded, and yet still-success-
ful, phrase.

Despite the color-blind efforts of those who speak in racial code, the
code's racialized meaning was clear to many residents. John, of Edgewater, discussed a community meeting he had recently attended:

> There was one meeting that I sat at that it was, we were all white, and
> we were talking about safety, and "these people," and "the element," and
> those words kept being used. . . . And I was sitting there somewhat quiet .
> . . finally somebody said, John, you've been very quiet, that's not typical of
> you, what are you thinking? And finally I said, I'm thinking I'm very un-
> comfortable sitting here, because if anyone ever heard this, I think they'd
> think we were a bunch of racists.

This code-breaking extended to a recent debate about retail in the bottom of a new development in the neighborhood: Franklin, of Edgewater,
said, "We had maybe a hundred people there, and just a lot of . . . people
were disappointed that an Aldi's, which they felt was a step in the wrong
direction because of the name of the Aldi's, the connotation of Aldi's is a
lower income type of name." Carla, also of Edgewater, also commented
on this code: "It's just the name, you know. And I'm sure the great German founder of Aldi is probably turning in his grave thinking that the
name, when you say Aldi, you think, like, slum, you know, grocery store."

Finally, perhaps the most infamous code among residents in these
communities is the term "gangbanger." While technically racially neutral in wording, it carries very strong racial connotations. Nine out of
41 residents used this term at one time or another, and although I did
not systematically include their posts in this study, it also has a vibrant
presence among the mostly-conservative or libertarian bloggers in these
communities. It also is a mobilizing element of community policing
strategies, as indicated by Matthew, of Rogers Park. Matthew had been
discussing progressive values in the community, and said:

> I was walking to work today and I noticed a flyer for a CAPS meeting, and
> the . . . meeting said come . . . learn about . . . problem buildings—bad
> tenants was the first bullet point. The second one was like gangs and
> crime. The third one was something else, like quality of life, generally
> speaking, and then the fourth one was subsidized housing.

And I thought to myself, why would you put out a flyer linking bad buildings and subsidized housing and gangs—as if those are all the same. . . . It's one thing to go to the meeting and someone say it. It's when the flyer—[*laughs*]—is put right out there saying this is about the problem buildings full of gangbangers who are in subsidized housing.

Many were careful about their language and worked to deliberately achieve political correctness alongside color-blindness in their codes. Angela, of Edgewater, had been discussing her first years in the neighborhood and her impressions of the community:

It's, um, certainly a mixed neighborhood where some streets being, uh, had been warned about absentee landlords, and uh, said "Be careful when you go down that street" and, where there was, you know, sort of a seemingly rougher clientele living on certain streets and others, you know, more kind of the university or professional looking people.

In her comments, Angela distinguishes between those who are "of a seemingly rougher clientele" and "university or professional looking people" rather than color-coding those populations for me.

Again, I cannot confirm the race of the residents, drug dealers, Section 8 Housing population, teenagers, hooligans, or rougher clientele in such discourse, specifically because this discourse is designed so that I am not able to do so. Jason Rodriquez has written about the flexibility in color-blind ideologies and their discursive frames, particularly in that this way of talking can incorporate "obviously racial markers and disassociate their connections with race" (2006, 663). Interviewees assumed that I would understand such codes, and indeed, as my linking strategies and fieldwork confirms, the codes were successful. This allowed the color-blind discourse to remain intact, especially as it was cohesive with a pro-diversity discourse. The next section explores how and when that marriage fails.

INCOHERENCE

Coded talk is significant for its ability to vividly communicate an idea or an opinion without directly discussing race. It is able to racialize

otherwise race-neutral discussion precisely because the code is shared
between talkers. The racialized elements of language are so familiar
that they remain overt and unspoken at the same time. However, the
existence of a color-blind society that is still deeply structured by race
creates contradictions that are not always so easy to capture in coded or
color-blind talk. This is especially so in communities like these, where
residents are both tremendously proud of their diverse community and
yet express, as the next chapter will show, deep ambivalence about the
policy and problems that relate to it. As Foster has noted, "whites walk
a discursive tightrope when discussing racial matters, and contradictions
appear throughout" (2009, 686). While there are certainly "well-rehearsed repertoires" (Steyn & Foster 208, 26) that speakers may employ
to remain complicit with the color-blind ideologies, there are also times
when that complicity is much more difficult to navigate. It is then that
speakers may lose their coherency.

While some scholars have dismissed incoherence as incomprehensible or the result of confusion (Bonilla-Silva 2003), I argue that this
discomfort or inability to speak clearly is not always a sign of bafflement
or an effort to conceal racism. Jane Hill notes: "Knowledge and ideas are
made available in discourse not simply through material presence [but
also] in absences. We can think of the material surface of discourse . . .
as partly a set of explicit articulations, but also as a set of suggestive gaps
that trigger inferences and connections among the stretches of explicit
utterance. So this analysis of discourse requires us to examine not only
what is said, but what is not said" (2008, 32).

Feminist scholars have made similar points about women and our use
of language. Specifically, Marjorie Devault has argued, " . . . the lack
of fit between women's lives and the words available for talking about
experience present real difficulties for ordinary women's self-expression
in their everyday lives" (1990, 97). I argue that the same is true for race
talk. Color-blind frames and racial codes present the "words available,"
and any desire to navigate outside of them is likely to invoke incoherence
among "ordinary" men and women, like those in this study. As such,
this incoherence, the ums and uhs that we may strategically ignore in
qualitative research, are rich in meaning. Again following Devault, "'You
know' no longer seems like a stumbling inarticulateness, but appears
to signal a request for understanding" (103). I argue that color-blind

ideology provokes the same request for understanding, especially among people who live in a diverse community, and it impacts their views about race and diversity. To further borrow from Devault, "What produces the analysis is the recognition that something is unsaid, and the attempt to articulate the missing parts of the account" (1990, 104).

Among the residents in this book, incoherence most often occurred when someone was otherwise willing to speak quite clearly about matters of race, including being willing to critique racism in others. Todd, of Rogers Park, was speaking about a lack of diverse networks in his community, despite the diverse demographics of the neighborhood. He did so in a sharply critical tone:

> I get invited to dinner parties and I'm thinking, "OK, knowing this person and what they do and all that." I go there and it's *all* white people, and it's all a discussion about condos. That's the powers that be [in this community] . . . . There's few places in this neighborhood that you really find a true diverse mixing of people in an everyday way . . .

Todd had been speaking so emphatically about this disconnect between others' appreciation for diversity and their own segregated networks, that I wrongly made the assumption that his own networks were racially diverse. When I asked him how he was able to do this differently, and integrate his social network, he had difficulty:

> Not so much, but um, (*pause*) it's changed over the years. Um. (*pause*) I— you know—and actually as much as it's changed, it's always sort of stayed the same. My networks have always been pretty inclusive, um, (*pause*) pretty inclusive. I mean, (*pause*) more and more. . . . Well, I shouldn't say more and more, but I think that's changed a little bit in the last 4 or 5 years, mostly because we don't seem to go out as much anymore. You know, I'm a little more homebound. Um.

I hadn't been trying to catch him in a contradiction. I had genuinely believed that he was different from the folks he criticized, and was eager to hear how he did things differently. Like many people, Todd had difficulty speaking directly and honestly about his own social networks. As scholars of privilege have noted, it is often easier to criticize others than to look critically and speak openly about our own life and relationships

(Thompson 2010). To do so would also require breaking from color-blindness, an ideal that many cherish and an ideology that many, as this chapter has shown, are unable to resist. These pressures disrupt his candidness about race in his own life. This is despite Todd being quite critical of racism in his community in other parts of our conversation. For the more complicated matter of personal networks, there was no code, no ideology or its easy frames, to make use of.

Another resident mirrored Todd's comments. Art, of Edgewater, had been speaking to me about the importance of integration to him and his family. He spoke eloquently about integration being both a moral and a practical necessity, not only for the neighborhood but also for the nation. Because integration seemed such a key element of his life choices in terms of housing and community, I asked him if he was successful in integrating his social network in his neighborhood:

> Not—not really a whole lot. Uh, we, uh, um, at, uh . . . well, I did, uh, I did in my work, of course, when I—well, we had, uh, we had some, uh, some African American employees with the accounting firm. And, uh, then, uh, of course when I got involved at [another workplace], that was, uh, a great deal of, uh, African Americans. This was in the '70s. And, uh, [my other job], again, the same way, so I was always working with, uh, integrated staff. But that was the main contact. We, uh, we had a, uh, mixed race couple live next door, uh, here for, uh, ten years, uh, ten of the years I've been here. We have, uh, uh, African American tenants at the—in the building next door here now, so it's, uh, we're—while we're, [I mean], we're speaking terms, we're not, uh, for whatever reason, uh, there's not an awful lot of social contact.

Here the overabundance of "uhs" and "ums" was distinctly different from his easy and comfortable speech patterns during the rest of our conversation. They express his discomfort in speaking frankly about race when it relates to his own life—a discomfort that is rooted in the pressure to adhere to a color-blind framework. As Devault (1990) notes, "In [cases like these], it may mean saying part of what is experienced, groping for words, doing the best one can. . . . As a researcher my job is to listen . . . and to analyze the disjunctures that give rise to them" (102).

While in the cases above I was asking about personal networks because the residents were so emphatic about the importance of integration in their communities and in their personal lives, incoherence also emerged when participants were discussing uncomfortable facts around particular events. Walter, of Uptown, had been discussing community efforts to decrease crime in his neighborhood, and mentioned a shooting that had recently taken place nearby:

> Unfortunately, one of the gang, uh, members got shot, uh, uh, uh, here because the gang is fighting between each other. And the sad part is it was only a 14-year-old, uh, boy. And, uh, the trouble is, uh . . . and those—some of the areas where our—you know, it's poverty. It's not racial, it's poverty. And they get into an issue where, uh, they're . . . sadly, a lotta those kids don't have a chance, and the gangs will recruit the young kids because they're a minority—not a minority—a minor. And, uh, they will, uh, they have some protection as a minor when they go to court, so they give them all the dirty jobs. So that's why this young kid got killed.

As was the case with the other examples, Walter was markedly more articulate and clear when speaking about most topics during our conversation. He was remarkably well-informed about gang activity in the area, and also the legal nuances of prosecuting and tracking crime in the courts after someone had been arrested. He spoke confidently and appreciatively about the value of diversity and the very careful measures community members were taking to effectively and responsibly fight crime. This coherence, however, lapsed when the topic moved to racialized issues. His nervousness about frankly discussing the facts of this shooting is structured by the color-blind ideologies which stand in the way of meaningful discourse and action. In fact, the strongest statement he made in the excerpt above was the line "It's not racial, it's poverty"—a common color-blind story line in the minimization of racism frame. That frame provided one branch to cling to in the otherwise unsteady waters of honest racial discussion.

These instances of incoherence were common in this study among residents who were being asked to either speak about race directly or about their own lives in racial terms. These were not bigots or racists who were trying to justify some kind of rash belief or action. Often the incoherence and uneasiness were related to facts of a specific event, the reality of a given situation, or very practical matters in their daily lives where there should be no need to exclude race from the conversation.

Race scholars have long critiqued the ways that color-blind ideologies stand in the way of meaningful discourse and action around race. This study indicates that even in racially diverse communities that have much more experience than the rest of the nation in directly dealing with matters of race, the color-blind mandate still can inhibit direct and meaningful talk and action.

COLOR-BLINDNESS, RACIAL CODES, AND INCOHERENCE

Coded talk is central to communication under a color-blind rubric, the strength of which is evident in this chapter. This code is structured by the ability of speakers to infer racial meaning into language that is specifically race-neutral. Rather than being off-limits to researchers, or available through expository journaling as in some prior studies (Myers 2005; Zamudio & Rios 2006), it is quite traceable through discussions with multiple persons, or by linking community evidence to racial discourse. While the fluency of these codes depends on inference rather than explicit language, they are important to consider as part of the color-blind universe of discourse. This chapter illuminates the deep racial meaning built into a color-blind framework, and the ability of speakers to navigate this racial ideology.

Racial codes are important not just for discourse analysis, but perhaps more significantly for their social function in a community—they answer the need to simultaneously discuss race and to adhere to the color-blind ideologies so strongly mandated by our popular culture in the United States. While contradictory in aim, both needs are important to the people I interviewed for this book. They are immersed and active in racially diverse communities, and yet still had trouble breaking from color-blind frames or speaking in anything other than the racial codes that uphold the color-blind norm. Race is a key element of these communities' diversity and identity, and linked in many residents' minds with some of its challenges. Unable to discuss those matters directly, coded talk helps them simultaneously uphold color-blindness and to discuss race.

This is what makes incoherence critical to appreciate. Bonilla-Silva has argued that incoherence is "part of the overall language of color-blindness" (2003, 54), yet he also asserts that responses like the ones above are "almost unintelligible" (ibid, 53). His work reveals the discursive structure to this ideology and asserts the role of color-blind ideologies that uphold white privilege in the contemporary U.S. While my findings do not disrupt his larger claim, the results of this study in a specific setting illuminate something other than "unintelligence." Instead, I expose the dual tensions that active residents committed to a diverse community must navigate in ways that can be quite savvy. Certainly such tensions are deeply racially loaded, and as the next chapter will detail, many privileges for whites remain intact through their discursive and community practices. After all, color-blindness inherently obscures the continuing significance of race in these communities. But not everyone in the community wants this to be the case. Instead, residents are uncertain how to move forward, and significantly, how to give meaningful voice to the very real racial dynamics within these communities. They need to talk about development, about housing issues, and about gangs, and they are by and large committed to the racial diversity in this community. Color-blindness leaves them trapped. Incoherence is their voice trying to escape.

While on the surface incoherent talk seems specifically void of meaning, it underscores the desire to say something outside of the bounds of legitimate discourse, something real and important to the actors in concrete environments. This is especially true among active residents of a diverse community, and uncovering this talk as significant has been central to my analysis in this chapter. As Bonilla-Silva's work illustrates, to date most researchers have assumed the talk we hear from participants in our studies to be complete and mobilized to uphold or preserve racism. Further, we have often failed to examine the dueling needs that people face in real rather than abstracted or hypothetical settings. I hope that this book adds to the understanding of the literatures around both residential integration and racial ideologies by examining such complex and contradictory dynamics in a real, dynamic setting.

Doing this is of critical importance because it can illuminate the link between racial ideologies and social action. The work of Bonilla-Silva, hugely influential in the race and ethnicity field, convincingly demonstrates the structure of color-blind ideology and its prevalence in the U.S. Similarly, coded talk has been shown to hold sway on college campuses (Myers 2005; Zamudio & Rios 2006), within an industry (Dirks & Rice 2004), and in multiple settings (Picca & Feagin 2006). Yet Omi and Winant make an important claim in their work, that "racial projects are always concretely framed, and thus are always contested and unstable" (2996, 58). Further, "to recognize the racial dimension in social structure is to interpret the meaning of race" (ibid, 57). Racial codes are key to this interpretation, as are the incoherence that their failure invokes, as it reveals the tension between racial ideology and social reality.

This is a tension that is constantly being negotiated not just in these residents' speech, but also in their community action. The next chapter reveals how residents consistently spoke supportively about the benefits of racial diversity and with frustration about those who disdain it. And yet as chapter 2 detailed and chapter 6 will further discuss, there is little concrete community action geared toward its preservation. Residents are actively involved in debates around development efforts, many types of safety initiatives, social events and historical preservation, and improving their collective city resources such as infrastructure and transit. While all such efforts impact the neighborhood landscape for its residents, these projects are more likely to stabilize the overrepresentation of whites who are homeowners rather than the less stable and, relative to community action, less visible minority renters. This is part of the re-creation of a white habitus inside these diverse communities, as the next chapter will reveal. While there are isolated community organizations actively trying to make racial diversity a priority, they have not had success. In the end, the negotiation of such tensions, in discourse and in action, remain equally ambivalent. And perhaps in communities such as these, more vividly than elsewhere, they illuminate the failures of color-blind approaches to the real and often complicated dynamics of racial diversity.

4

CONSUMING DIVERSITY

While the last chapter explored the ways that color-bind ideologies hold influence in liberal, racially diverse communities, and the ways that residents struggled to speak through those frames, this chapter is devoted to discussions of diversity: how it is discussed and prioritized within the community. Specifically, I argue that discussion around diversity both reveals and reproduces what sociologists call a white habitus inside of these diverse communities. A habitus is essentially a framework or set of often unexamined assumptions that structure thinking and acting in everyday life. A white habitus is one that couples neatly with normative whiteness in a given context to uphold white privileges, here the context of U.S. race relations. This habitus is complicit with color-blind ideologies, but a habitus is rarely articulated in familiar ways such as in the frames of color-blind racism. Instead, it determines thought and action in less visible ways, while still re-creating the normative space and privileges for those in the norm through social action.

This chapter reveals the link between racial discourse and social action, a process Omi and Winant call a racial project: "A racial project is simultaneously an interpretation, representation, or explanation of racial dynamics, and an effort to reorganize and redistribute resources along particular racial lines" (1994, 56). These reorganizations and redistributions do not always take place on a national or global scale, nor are those resources necessarily economic in nature. They are also part of our negotiation process in everyday interactions. "Racial projects connect what race means in a particular discursive practice and the ways in which both social structures and everyday experiences are racially *organized*, based upon that meaning" (ibid). In short, ideas about race produce real social outcomes. Closely examining this process in a racially diverse urban community makes this connection visible in ways that help us better understand the link between discourse and social action more generally. Fundamentally, they expose a gap between desired and achieved outcomes. Residents appreciate living in a diverse community, but often unintentionally act in ways that may undermine it.

Understanding this dynamic in an often-celebrated diverse community is of critical importance. As Bonilla-Silva, Lewis, and Embrick note: "Racial outcomes . . . are not the product of individual 'racists' but of the crystallization of racial domination into a racial structure" (2004, 558). Several authors have linked this to the perpetuation of what Bonilla-Silva calls a white habitus. Borrowing on Bourdieu, Bonilla-Silva defines white habitus as "a racialized, uninterrupted socialization process that conditions and creates whites' racial taste, perceptions, feelings, and emotions and their views on racial matters" (2003, 104). Bonilla-Silva and Embrick's (2007) work specifically considered the link between a white habitus and the simultaneous perpetuation of prejudice toward blacks and privileges for whites. However, where they focused on the impact of extreme racial segregation, I look at the creation and recreation of a white habitus in a racially integrated environment. Closely examining the white habitus that can operate in a racially diverse community is of critical importance, for it exposes the faulty link between color-blind ideals and social realities, namely the influence of market forces and struggles over social problems like crime in the community.

These color-blind ideologies are often articulated in the form of race talk, "specific linguistic ways of articulating racial views" (Bonilla-Silva 2001, 61). This race talk varies by topic and locale, but as scholars of discourse have long noted, is "intimately involved in the construction and maintenance of inequality" (Foster 2009, 13). The race talk around diversity, as Bell and Hartmann (2007) have shown, manifests in "happy talk" around the idea of diversity. This well-rehearsed repertoires, or conceptual frameworks (Frankenburg 1999), celebrate diversity as universally positive. But as Bell and Hartmann demonstrate, this idea is exactly that—universalized and often disconnected from our daily lives. As the talk moves from the abstract to the concrete, happiness disappears and discussions of challenges and frustrations emerge. This is similar to my analysis of incoherence in chapter 3. Here I examine how these frustrations can stem from the contradictions between a consumption-based approach to diversity embraced by many in the contemporary United States, and the very real problems that are encountered in everyday life. Perhaps for this reason, rather than commit to diversity via racial or social justice efforts, the active residents in these communities reproduce a white habitus in a racially diverse space. By maintaining what Bell and Hartmann call a white normative center, the assumption that diversity is an add-on to an otherwise "normal" white experience, residents also reproduce a white habitus. Their ideal of living in a diverse community is subverted by the realities that they produce in their actions—a color-blind, power-neutral approach to individual and collective community action. This allows these residents to retain diversity as a positive in the abstract while treating it with caution and ambivalence on the ground.

This process is in some ways similar to what Picca and Feagin (2007) call "Two-Faced Racism." Their concept borrows heavily on Goffman and his analysis of front and back stages. That is, many whites may participate in socially acceptable discourse around race in public, but maintain overt racism or discrimination when out of the public view. My study differs from theirs in that I find ambivalence and contradictions in the back stage, or what I call the individualized and community forms of social action. This may be due to the fact that I was interviewing active residents of diverse communities, many of whom are liberal and quite genuinely eager to accept and nurture diversity. This makes their ambivalence and contradictions, when discourse is filtered down into individual and community action, all the more important to critically analyze. As Foster has noted, "built into habitus is the ability to shift gears in one's status with the superstructure of society" (2009, 696). Attention to these contradictions, the ways in which well-intentioned individuals stumble over the cracks produced by this ideological and discursive system, are likely to be all the more pertinent as the nation itself becomes more diverse.

My evidence for the production of white habitus is broken down into three sections, which mirror progressive stages in the link between ideologies and actions. I liken this process to a hurricane making landfall. Fueled by ideology, the discourse is strong and confident, sweeping far in its reach, and having a universalized impact on a local setting. This is the universal happy talk in a local setting that I detail in the first section. But as the storm moves inland, its strength weakens. Very much still impacted by the storm, the inner coastal region of individual action enacts diversity as individualized choice and action. For a site like mine, this is captured by the everyday ways in which individuals "do" diversity via choice and consumption. Finally, the storm weakens when it moves to the central landmass of social action. Here the discursive storm finally breaks apart, and residents are left dealing with the larger-scale decisions in the real estate market and in community issues, both of which have a strong impact on the community and its diversity. In fact, it works to weaken it, as ambivalent social action around matters related to diversity and individual economic preservation are placed above intentional community efforts.

PRO-DIVERSITY HAPPY TALK

This section explores the race talk in these communities, "specific linguistic ways of articulating racial views" (Bonilla-Silva 2001, 61). As Bell and Hartmann (2007) have shown, the pressure is very strong throughout the nation to celebrate diversity as a universal positive through what they call "happy talk." This "happy talk" is not a stretch for the active members of these communities, who enthusiastically embrace the community's identity as diverse, even if, as a later section in this chapter will show, they are uneasy about some of the challenges that this brings. In fact, I did not interview anyone for this book who did not speak about the neighborhood's diversity as a positive feature. A comment by Fred, of Rogers Park, was particularly revealing in this regard: "Here in Rogers Park, even if you don't believe in diversity, you certainly know you better sound like you do, okay?" Fred's comment indicates that while throughout the nation the pressure to celebrate diversity is strong, in these communities, breaking from that happy talk would also undermine the identity of these neighborhoods as tolerant, progressive places.

It also helps residents embrace a personal identity that is appreciative of diversity in part by living within a community that embraces it, as chapter 5 explores in more detail. For example, Laurie, of Rogers Park, had been discussing her involvement with a local political campaign and said:

> Through my involvement in that [campaign], I learned more about different challenges in the area, and learned just really what a valuable jewel Rogers Park is in terms of being known nationally as one of the most diverse congressional districts or communities in the country. And that made me feel even better about living here, so . . .

Yet just because the link is strong between diversity and the identity of these communities does not mean that many residents are able to discuss it in anything other than abstract terms.

When I met Walter, of Uptown, he spoke immediately about the value he places on diversity, yet he connected it to his work life rather than home. When I asked him to talk more about why diversity was such an appeal for him, he said:

> It's a very tough issue when you talk to some people where they get over the hump on it and realize it's a value. And I see diversity as a plus, in a sense. All great things come from the edge of a paradigm, and when you have a diverse workforce, a diverse body of people, they're all thinking different ways, so their paradigm's sounding different. So I think you come up with better ideas, more creative, with diversity. And it's more interesting.

Despite being someone who spoke several times during our conversation about the value he places on diversity in his community, his emphasis on cultural difference and paradigm shifts does not use his home community as a basis for his discussion. Ellis and Wright (2004) have shown that it is much more common for people to have diverse interactions in their workplace than at home. Indeed, as some of the incoherence demonstrated in the previous chapter, Walter was not the only one who found it easier to connect across the color line at work, or even in principle, than at home.

While universally positive about the idea of diversity and its intrinsic value, be it at work or at home, it was also very common for residents to immediately expand the notion of diversity far beyond race, to emphasize the community's extra-racial diversity. This allows for the maintenance of "happy talk," and a diminished emphasis on race, which is complicit with color-blind ideologies. Shannon, of Rogers Park, had been talking about her comfort in the community and emphasized:

> Yeah, and I think it's diverse in a lot of ways. Not just race. I mean the age thing makes a huge—the generational thing is huge, or your agenda in life, having family or not having a family. There's a lot of people who do have kids or don't and that's a huge experience for those people that have very different interests.

Expansive lists naming what diversity means were common among residents in these communities, reminding me of racial diversity lists that eventually incorporate green and blue. This list-making serves a peculiar ideological function, as it accurately understands that diversity is not just about race, while at the same time listing so many elements that the racial component, which specifically defines this community, is easily lost. Diversity itself becomes color-blind.

This is part of the process of creating a white habitus in these communities, as race is typically not the buy-in for individual whites around diversity. Prior research has demonstrated that most whites do not see race as something critical to their identities and experiences (see Perry 2001; Myers 2005). Emphasizing nonracial difference allows them to maintain a white core of identity in the community, a phenomenon further examined in chapter 5. It also provides further evidence that even in liberal, diverse communities like these, diversity still remains personalized rather than political, and often unchecked given its extra-racial nature. Diversity loses both its political currency and its racial associations.

Some residents recognized that lost meaning, playing with the term and its importance while at the same time accounting for the realities in these communities, as John, of Edgewater, does here when criticizing his block club's mission statement:

You know, "it's the mosaic of our diverse community" blah-blah-blah. We are a diverse community. There is a strong Balkan population there. We have a large gay community there. We have a large retired community. We've got homeowners versus condo owners versus high-rises, which present their own unique challenges. I don't think renters get a lot of attention. So you've got a lot of different kinds of diversity. And then you've got some other ethnic diversity in the community.

His use of the word "mosaic" followed by "blah-blah-blah" suggests that, for him, the idea of diversity has become cliché. His comment, I think, critiques that co-optation. Yet at the same time, he also chooses to emphasize the nonracial elements of diversity, a point explored further in the next chapter. This is despite other points in our conversation where he was sharply critical of the community for some of its racist undertones.

While appreciative of the range of identities that diversity does indeed contain, this popular sentiment worked to diminish the significance of race contained in "diversity" through the very process of celebrating it. While in Bell and Hartmann's (2007) study participants also generated expansive lists for what is contained within "diversity," here that reality gains potency, particularly as it is enacted by whites who hold disproportionate power in shaping community action. Residents lack what Twine and Steinbugler call racial literacy, which is defined as "an everyday practice—an analytic stance that facilitates ongoing self-education and enables members . . . to translate racial codes, decipher racial structures, and manage the racial climate in their local and national communities" (2006, 344). This is similar to Frankenburg's (1999) conception of race cognizance, which insists on the importance of understanding difference politically rather than through essentialist terms. This racial literacy or race cognizance is a critical void among residents who hold the reigns in these racially diverse communities. Lacking that, as diversity is both celebrated in the abstract and expanded in its ingredients, community discussions and action preserve a white habitus, which, following Bonilla-Silva and Embrick (2007), facilitates little interracial contact and does not provoke whites to see this gap as a problem. It is the essence of what Margaret Andersen (1999) has famously called "diversity without oppression." There is no discussion of problems or inequalities in happy talk that might rock the boat, nor does there exist a challenge to whites in the community to consider their own racial position in relation to community dynamics. Unchallenged and firmly centered in the discourse within these communities, particularly for those active residents whose views and actions shape the community on a daily basis, privileges for whites and a secure white habitus remain intact.

CONSUMING DIVERSITY

The next step in the racial project linking ideology to social action follows the happy and diffused discourse discussed above in ways that also sustain a white habitus. Primarily because diversity is seen as something A) extraracial and B) as a positive add-on to a white normative center, residents' concrete experiences around "diversity" are individually focused and consumption-driven. Much like in the national study of happy talk by Bell and Hartmann (2007), diversity is perceived as something extra, rather than integrated into the core of a community, making diversity particularly appealing to whites who are looking to spice up or add flavor to an otherwise unexamined white normative life. It is something that they consume rather than engage in the process of community. And they do so by enacting individual choice, a hallmark of racial privilege. This freedom of choice easily translates into consumption, so much so that consumption becomes the key way that diversity is "done" (West & Zimmerman 1987) in the community.

This may be particularly disappointing given the hope invested in stably diverse communities. As chapter 6 will discuss, all of the literature on stable racial integration suggests that intentional, community-driven processes are key to developing and sustaining diversity therein. However, the outcomes from experiences in diverse communities are far less clear. Integrated settings like schools and neighborhoods do not necessarily translate into diverse social networks like friendships or intimate relationships (Emerson, Kimbro, & Yancey 2002). Indeed, as discussed above, work is more likely than home to be a place where interracial or other intergroup interaction takes place (Ellis & Wright 2004). While diversity is enthusiastically embraced, it is consumed on an individual basis rather than engaged in meaningful relationships or in intentional community action.

In the design of this research, I wanted to gain an understanding of what diversity meant to the active members of these neighborhoods by discussing their concrete experiences, not asking them to fill in a survey or define or discuss diversity in the abstract, as many prior studies have done. For that reason, I only asked them details about their process of engaging diversity within the neighborhood if they claimed that diversity was a central issue for them in the community. Indeed, most did. Yet when I asked those same people what they appreciate about living in a diverse community, "ethnic" restaurants, religious sites, and stores were the most common responses. This was also true in the national study conducted by Bell and Hartmann: "Whether pegged to music, food, clothes, or some other aspect of consumption, an expanded range of choice is not only the most concrete but also the most common benefit of diversity our respondents had to offer" (2007, 900). Residents in these communities are not engaging diversity in ways that radically alter the normative center of a white habitus, even given their location in a liberal, diverse community. Instead, they are valuing and relating to diversity in the same ways as those in the rest of the country who are living in segregated communities.

For example, Rick and I were well into our interview when he mentioned how Rogers Park is known nationally for its diversity. I said, "Right. And is that something that—that's something that you hadn't mentioned yet," and he interjected:

Rick: Well I get off on the fact that I can get a lot of different products here that are unique to the world. Or that, I guess they're not available elsewhere.

MAB: Uh huh. Such as?

Rick: Um, soaps. I can go to Devon Avenue, I can do my grocery shopping and get fabulous produce. And nobody knows this but like the people that live around there. So if you prefer to go to Dominick's, I understand, and why you'd wanna go there to get Tony-O's pizzas. But you can't get those on Devon. So that's the choice that I have here.

Consuming goods like soaps and other products functioned as a proxy for more meaningful action that would sustain the community's diversity among its residents. This is true even if it still had individual value for the residents. Erin, of Rogers Park, spoke about this as a feeling of connection that this diverse community provides through this consumption:

> *Erin:* I just wanna feel connected to people like myself and also people unlike myself. You know, I'm drawn to this [at work], I'm drawn to—I've lived in [other parts of the world], working there. I like being surrounded by people [who] are different than me, and can share their culture with me. I think it makes for a richer community basically.
>
> *MAB:* Mm hmm. And so what are some ways that you are able to do that in the neighborhood?
>
> *Erin:* Well you know, there's restaurants that you can eat at. But it's even just like you're down at the park and here's a guy and he's from Ethiopia, and he's a refugee, and he's got his daughter, and you have a conversation, you know.

Responses like Erin's, which were common, share the literal meaning of consumption as something to take in or ingest, and in many cases something to benefit from rather than share in or give back. The emphasis most often is on consumption of "diversity" as an achieved benefit for individuals rather than as a process of community formation. Diversity is insulated to individual experiences, not making its way into relationships in the community. Only 3 of the 41 residents I interviewed mentioned a significant interracial friendship or romantic relationship; two of these were discussing each other. This is even the case, as Todd's example below illustrates, for those who are otherwise most committed to diversity:

> I get invited to dinner parties and I'm thinking, "OK, knowing this person and what they do and all that." I go there and it's *all* white people, and it's all a discussion about condos. That's the powers that be [in this community]. That's the people that are going to meetings that are involved in politics, whether trying to unseat an elected official or [working as] an ally of. . . . There's few places in this neighborhood that you really find a true diverse mixing of people in an everyday way . . .

Diversity as an achieved benefit rather than community formation may enhance the individual lives of those who consume it as such, but it does not alter the additive model, which keeps individual achievement and normative whiteness at the center of a white habitus and adds diversity as enhancement or accessory from there.

The same process holds true when there is an emphasis on communing through food, especially when it is discussed in abstracted, future terms, as was the case with Carla, of Uptown:

> *MAB:* And you've talked a couple times sort of in passing about the diversity being an appeal. Can you talk a little bit more about what that meant for you and how you can kind of connect to that?
>
> *Carla:* Food. [*laughs*] Food and music I think are the big. . . . Food and music and languages. I just think that those things can bring us—they can separate us, but they can bring us together, too. . . . And I just thought the kids need to be exposed to that. They need—food has always been important to us, too, and diversity of food, of quote, unquote, "ethnic" food, I mean, if you can call it, but it's not ethnic to them. I mean, you know what I mean? . . . I think if we could just all eat together and have a party, you know, I mean, we might really appreciate each other and understand a little bit more about the cultural advances and that kind of thing.

While Carla's point contains a more concrete emphasis on community than the other individual-based responses, and also espouses the hope contained in what is called the "contact hypothesis," that interracial contact will lessen hostility and tension, it remains just that, a hope.

It is here that we see another window into what Bonilla-Silva and Embrick have called the "apparent 'paradox' between whites' commitment to the principle of interracialism and their mostly white pattern of association" (2007, 327). As Hughey noted in his study of people of color in white sororities and fraternities, "when studying instances of racial 'integration' we must not only examine access to resources . . . [but also] how robust white supremacist schema constrain and enable the interpretation of that access and those resources" (2010, 674). In short, Hughey argues, we must not treat integration as "the successful end, [but rather] a problematic beginning of analysis" (ibid, 653). Twine and Steinbugler note a similar problematic, in that "intimate relationships with Blacks neither guarantees nor are sufficient to catapult one across the chasm of . . . color-blindness" (2006, 344). In short, as this chapter demonstrates, the mere numerical presence of an integrated population does not guarantee that those within are not living lives structured along racial lines.

Further, the reality is that these restaurants, stores, and to a lesser extent religious sites are vital elements of these neighborhoods' stable diversity given their role in supporting their ethnic, national, and, in some cases, racial constituents. They are for this reason locations frequented by a diverse group of residents in the neighborhood. While going to an Ethiopian restaurant and dining at tables near people from all sectors of the community may be a pleasurable experience for individual consumers, it is not the same as building relationships and doing the hard work of community development. This is again where I take a strong departure from Elijah Anderson's argument in his recent book about cosmopolitan canopies. He writes, "When diverse people are eating one another's food, a social good is performed for those observing. As people become intimate through such shared experiences, some barriers can be broken" (2011, 33–34). Yet as Moody reminds us, "simple exposure does not *promote* integration [emphasis mine]" (2001, 707). Therefore part of the challenge, even in its positivity, is in how residents see eating at these restaurants or buying these soaps "doing diversity." Consumption becomes sufficient for engaging diversity, rather than a step toward investing in it more fully. This problem is perhaps only enhanced by community efforts geared toward development, beautification, and crime fighting in these communities, all of which support this market rather than focusing together on affordable housing or school improvement that would enhance the diverse community for all.

The same trend also was common in residents' talk about public spaces, beyond restaurants and stores. The fact that appreciating diversity in extra-economic venues was still tied to a sense of consuming, of taking in, and of scene-setting, again much like in Elijah Anderson's recent book (2011), details how deeply entrenched this particular form of "doing diversity" has become. Like Erin above, many participants spoke about the general feeling of goodness that came from seeing something other than white faces on the sidewalk, white bodies on the beach, or white folks in the parks. Walter, of Uptown, tied this to urban, cosmopolitan life in general:

> So that's a lot of the fun of the city is you can get all the diversity, you can walk, you got the park. Take a ride and down the park and you see all

kinds of different people, meet different people. So I think that's the fun
of living in the city.

It is easy here to imagine scenes in a film, landscapes flashing past a car
window; in either case the emphasis is not on interaction but on scenery.
This is the crux of Elijah Anderson's concept of "cosmopolitanism, by
which I mean acceptance of the space as belonging to all kinds of people" (2011, 5). It is passive and like those examples of literal consumption above, it is still centered on, and to the benefit of, the individual.
Further, these are not just any individuals in the community, but those
who are most powerful, and mostly middle-class property owners. Even
many of Anderson's spaces are "mostly white and middle class with a
healthy mix of people of color" (2011, 32). Anderson also repeatedly
notes tolerance as key to the success of cosmopolitan canopies. Yet as
Wellman notes, "tolerance is not simply an attribute middle-class people
learn; it is also a luxury they can afford . . . because the questions are so
posed that the issues raised have no direct meaning for these people"
(51). Given this conceptual and emotional distance, it was rare to hear
this scenery work its way into personal interactions.

That personal interaction, even when limited, was still abstracted, as
Eric's case illustrates. Eric, of Edgewater, had been talking about how
he is able to build a diverse set of relationships in the community, and
said:

> I think in the community itself, too, we've met just a very diverse, broad
> group of people. Um, and like I said, it's a big walking outside community,
> so you meet, you know, people on the beach, and some people you see in
> October and then you don't see them on the beach again until you know,
> May or whatever. And they could have dogs or they could have kids, or
> they could have neither, but you just see them and say hi, what have
> you been up to. And sometimes you don't even know their name, either.
> That's kind of the cool thing about it. But you know them. And you care
> about what they've been up to.

Eric does describe interactions that he codes as diverse, but they are still
quite generalized, and to an extent superficial, as evidenced by his emphasis on faces, the seasonal aspect of the interactions, and not knowing
people's names. He does care about the people he meets in this context,

but his response still falls into the category of consumption rather than community-building, given its surface-level content.

Again this is echoed in Anderson's work:

> On occasion strangers engage in spontaneous conversation, getting to know one another. Testing others and trying things out on them, people want to find out whether those different from themselves are sincere; happily, many discover that they are. People generally leave these encounters with a good feeling about one another, as though recognizing that they have experienced something profound. Indeed, they have—they have made human contact across the assumed barriers of race, ethnicity, and other differences (2011, 38).

Where Anderson is hopeful about these interactions persuading people that "these particularities" really do not matter (2011, 58), I am critical of the ways that they may enhance the lives of whites more so than people of color, by making them feel good, without producing more socially just outcomes for people of color or a sustained commitment to diversity for the community as a whole. Even Anderson asks, "Why is it that the black male seems to stress the fabric of the canopy . . .?" (2011, 141), and goes on to say, "When dark-skinned visitors approach the canopy and begin to partake of its wondrous social benefits, they are tolerated, even sometimes embraced, provided they exhibit 'good behavior,' but they may have to endure an extra measure of scrutiny by their hosts" (2011, 155–56). What else reveals the white habitus inside diverse spaces more than that statement about "tolerance" and dark-skinned "visitors" by "their hosts"? After all, Bonilla-Silva and Embrick (2007) have noted that "whites' extreme racial isolation from blacks does not provide a fertile soil upon which primary interracial associations can flourish regardless of blacks' level of assimilation" (341). This site of a racially integrated community steered by liberal, pro-diversity whites makes that isolation, and the resulting recreation of a white habitus, particularly vivid.

Further, this consumption was not only limited to white residents, a fact which demonstrates the reality that a white habitus is also something that people of color can incorporate and reproduce. Anthony, who is not white, described similar sentiments:

It just makes it interesting to live around and see the Sudanese from Africa. On Sundays, along the lakefront, to see the Russian seniors walking along like it's the promenade. They dress nicely and they just stroll. And you can just tell they did this in their country, too. And it's just like living in a different country. I think it's beneficial for all to see that.

I think it broadens your mind and your horizons and it makes you want to—it makes me want to see more and experience more and get to know people. And I think sometimes when you see, when people are at ease, sometimes you'll see the Russian seniors watching the black guys play basketball on the lakefront, because they're just sitting there watching the guys. You know, they're just learning from, just that type of interaction brings people together. And it's not one big love fest. But people can coexist together, just as long as there's mutual respect and standards. Respect for other people and their space.

Anthony's sentiments strongly echo Elijah Anderson's assertions about the canopy, but I am not completely cynical about their potential to open minds and foster further contact and cooperation. For example, it is important to note that all residents who spoke this way expressed a desire to see this site serve as a potential space for community. However, that site remains untested in most interactions. It seems that even in diverse communities, residents do not have the tools or community strategies to support and sustain such efforts. Instead, they are doing diversity alone.

Diverse communities are not immune to the national forces that emphasize individualism and consumption as a primary means of identity and community (Putnam 2000). Indeed, those same elements are at the core of a comfortable white habitus, even in a diverse community. Further, they may be working against the hopeful, abstracted intentions of residents in these communities by restructuring emotional segregation, "an institutionalized process whereby [whites] are unable to see people of color as emotional equals or as capable of sharing the same human emotions and experiences" (Beeman 2007, 687). After all, individualism and consumption are at the core of market forces that are a continual threat to diverse communities. What else is gentrification if not the importing of a white habitus into a formerly diverse or nonwhite space? If residents are not taking a more active stand in fighting to sustain the racial diversity of these communities through antigentrification and pro-sustenance efforts, they will likely lose the diversity that they are so happy to consume and claim.

AMBIVALENCE: REALTY AND REALITY

As the above sections demonstrated, diversity was actively embraced as an ideal among the residents I interviewed. They also found "diversity" to be a source of personal enjoyment, especially by consuming it. However, further discussion about both neighborhood challenges and personal assets eroded this positive discourse. This is not to say that the residents' views about diversity were negative once the surface of discourse and personal enjoyment was scratched, but that beneath this surface there exists a deep ambivalence and, understandably given our culture that promotes it, a priority for one's personal success above that of the community. It is this final link in the chain between ideology, discourse, and social action that ultimately reproduces a white habitus in this racially diverse community. Where the above sections explored the happy talk surrounding diversity generally, and the consumption-based practices that support it for individuals in daily life, this section will examine the ways in which diversity often does not find support in community action or in individual priorities. Specifically in the worlds of real estate and community action, where very real problems are addressed in the community and individual families make choices that impact their family and financial future, the happy discourse tends to fade, while the color-blind ideologies and individual focus remain strong. The result is an ongoing reshaping of the community in ways that protect comfort and privileges for whites, even if they are not often directly antagonistic toward people of color in the community.

Realty

I asked each resident I interviewed why they had chosen to move into the community. While diversity almost always made the list of favorable features in the neighborhood upon entry, residents would often eventually distill the important factors down to their essentials: the trinity of affordable housing (be it renting or owning), proximity to the lake, and proximity to transit. That is, while residents actively participate in diversity's "happy talk," it's rarely what brought or keeps them in these communities. When I asked Erin, of Rogers Park, what she most appreciated about her community, she answered, "Um, I like the proximity to the lake. I like that it's a diverse community and an old community, you know, its old buildings. Those are probably my top three." Anthony gave me his list when I had simply asked where he had lived: "I moved to Uptown, and I liked it. Diversity, by the lake, good public transportation. . . . The same things I like about Uptown, diversity, lakefront, transportation, I like about Edgewater." Further, despite the emphasis on diversity in many parts of the discussion with everyone I interviewed, diversity was absent from discussions about real estate.

When I asked Rick how he made the choice to buy his condo in Rogers Park rather than elsewhere in the city, he answered:

> Well, I was—again, with price. I mean, it's a wise move because there is an upside here that you don't see in a lot of communities. I could get a place that was reasonably priced, yet near the lake, with high in and out for still a good price. So that's why I stayed.

Residents spoke with a sense that these communities are hidden gems for buying or renting a home in the city, and they appreciate the combination of amenities and affordability that they provide. Indeed, these communities do provide some of the best prices for rental or sale in the city, and the proximity to Lake Michigan, its parks, and transit is better than most other parts of Chicago. It should be emphasized that those for whom diversity isn't of driving importance on the real estate front were not necessarily adverse to diversity. Rather, their comments reveal that for all diversity's happy talk, it is not often a central feature of the neighborhood for even its most active residents. Their emphasis is on the neighborhood's material amenities. These communities, like most others, are shaped primarily by market forces.

At other times talk about amenities was a stated departure from diversity's "happy talk," which only underlines the discursive front on which so much of the community dynamics take place. Todd, of Rogers Park, acknowledged the idealism of diversity as a lucky circumstance rather than a driving feature in his choice to move or stay in the community:

> I immediately knew I was staying here, and here I'll waive the cliché flag,
> A) because of its diversity and B) because of the lake. And on any given

day I could say that the lake is by far the reason I've stayed over *just* about anything. Because the people have changed and moved, and you know, you learn a little bit more about a place and its dynamics, but the lake is truly one thing that has drawn me here.

The acknowledgment of diversity as cliché from Todd is revealing. He knows that many residents name diversity as a defining feature of the neighborhood and something to speak positively about. And indeed he values it as well, as one of the two main reasons that he loves the neighborhood. But having said that, he admits that the lake is the thing that's really kept him there. The gap opened by this discourse allows more typical market forces, which do not deliberately sustain diversity in collective social or political action, to reveal themselves.

There was other talk about choices to move to or remain in the neighborhood that illuminate these fault lines. Adam, of Uptown, was discussing his choice to move to his community and said:

> But that was really more the yard than anything else, I mean, to be honest with you. It was trying to satisfy our needs of how do we stay in the city, have a house with a yard that we can afford, and still, as a gay couple, feel like we're not the odd couple out. And again, this neighborhood fit all of those qualifications for us.

While for this couple being in a diverse neighborhood that was not adverse to gay homeownership is vitally important, the yard was still a central element to this purchase, as his "honest" talk reveals. Others leveled the conversation with the word "honest'" as well. Wendy, of Rogers Park, answered my question about how she decided to move from a nearby community to her neighborhood as follows: "Well, it was because I wanted to buy a condo. And honestly, the initial part of that was really because it was more affordable than [it was there]."

There is also a considerable amount of ambivalence connected to what residents see as downsides of the community. These may be the sites where the white habitus is most actively maintained. As Shannon, of Rogers Park, said:

> I guess I don't know that I see myself living in [this community] for the rest of my life. Definitely I didn't see this as "OK you're going to move

[there] and stay in [there]." I never did. I think I see myself as the kind of person that would probably get married and have kids and want them to go to a certain school. And I'm not sure that I think all the schools are that great. I don't know.

Concern over the public schools is widespread among residents in all three neighborhoods I studied, and indeed almost all of the residents I spoke with chose to send their children to parochial rather than public schools, making the schools a central factor in their choice to remain in the neighborhood. In the end, housing choices do not significantly center around diversity, but rather more traditional real-estate calculations. Further, the perceived risks of living in a diverse community were a continual part of this calculation. It also drove the community action that protected and upheld white habitus, as I detail below.

Reality

Tracing the link between discourse and social action allows us to examine the relative strength of the competing values present within any ideological system. For example, color-blindness maintains several tenets: the tacit idea that race shouldn't matter, the idea that in fact it no longer does, and the idea that individualism is the defining value in all social and political contexts. Color-blindness is certainly ideological in that it specifically takes racism off the table for analysis and discussion, as explored in chapter 3. But it is also, like any ideology, an effort to make sense of ideas that are not alone coherent in all settings.

I interviewed residents about multiple aspects of their lives, especially the choice to move into a diverse community, the things that may cause them to leave, and their concrete work in the community. In the space of those discussions, the ideology and the discourse through which the ideology speaks was tested in ways that allowed me as a researcher to better understand those fault lines. I can discover where diversity is easier for people to accept and embrace, and where it is more challenging as people try to make sense of their community and their world. After all, it is in the context of that belief system where choices about residence and community action are made. In particular, diversity made the discursive cut when residents were speaking broadly about neighborhood values and how they appreciate their community. The section above demonstrated how they will happily incorporate it into their consumptive choices, and chapter 5 explores how it is also linked to the racial identities of whites. Yet diversity also was linked to the things that they found challenging about the community, including in extreme cases what might prompt them to leave.

The complexity and ambivalence that residents expressed around diversity disrupts their own happy talk, but also echoes the uncertainty that many people all over the nation face when diversity moves from an abstract ideal down into one's lived experiences. As Bell and Hartmann note: "Respondents typically define diversity in broad and inclusive terms, but when asked to describe personal experiences with difference, their responses are almost exclusively tied to race. . . . Therefore, although 'diversity' may sound race-neutral . . . the discourse of diversity is deeply racialized" (2007, 905). Walter, of Uptown, had been talking about community efforts to fight crime and said:

> Well, I think people that live in the area, in general, I think there's a lot of the people that enjoy the diversity of [this community], and celebrate that. But there's other people that moved here and still have racial fears and fear of the . . . somebody different. And that's always gonna be around. The only way . . . the best way is if you can have a diverse society, you find that well, "he looks different, but jeez, he's not any different. He's not so frightening." And, uh, so that helps.
>
> But I'd say in general, there's more people here that are . . . I think enjoy the diversity than a lotta other places. . . . But it's a growing experience. It will take years and years more. We're getting better. I think it's a lot better than what we had, but we're not home free yet.

Residents like Walter are acknowledging that crime, or more often perceptions thereof, are also an element of these neighborhoods' identities. In fact, his link between the perception of diversity, race, and crime are quite clear in his comments. His response struggles to construct a narrative around diversity that is simultaneously positive and realistic. This desire is not often reconcilable with some of the social realities residents encounter, which they understand in deeply racialized ways. As Frankenburg has shown in her study of those who make an effort not to see racial difference, "a number of strategies for talking about race and culture emerged, effectively dividing the discursive terrain into areas of 'safe' and 'dangerous' differences, 'pleasant' and 'nasty' differences, and generating modes of talking about difference that evaded questions of power" (1999, 149).

These responses were common when residents discussed the challenges in the community. Erin, of Rogers Park, said:

> [This] is known to be a community where there's a lot of crime, a lot of violence, a lot of gang activity. This summer I was walking back from the beach and I stepped in a syringe in the middle of the street. You know, it's like—it's not a perfect community. There's a lot of people with severe persistent mental illness who live up here, and there are social services agencies.
>
> I don't mean it's not perfect, I mean I think there's complications you— not only you benefit from the diversity that's here, you know, there's also challenges I think associated. Um, there are certain parts of [this neighborhood] where I just wouldn't walk by myself at night. And certainly wouldn't feel comfortable when my child's older having him walk around.

There were some residents who resisted this ambivalence, and told me about times when they worked to disrupt the discourse of racialized fear in conversations with others, while still extolling the positives of living in a diverse community. Todd had been talking about the challenges in attracting businesses to [the community], and said, "I've met plenty of people who, over the years, 'Oh, you live [there], isn't that dangerous? A lot of black people.' (pause) You know." While Todd went on to explain his challenge to such coded language and its racialized assumptions, his account reveals these neighborhoods, and the discourses surrounding them, to be sites of negotiation and challenges, not of a uniform positivity that the broader diversity discourse would suggest.

Oftentimes residents were able, even in color-blind terms, to speak about how they have negotiated their relationship to the community in light of this "downside" of diversity. Hank, of Uptown, explained his decision to move into his community as follows:

> I looked at Uptown . . . with one eye closed because of the remembrances of all the homeless walking the streets and people sleeping on the curbs and things like that, and knowing the history of that. That's the thing that

got me, if I can keep the gang bangers, drug guys away from my community, that's all I can offer. And then hopefully the next group down pushes them further someplace else, but you'll never get rid of them, you know. I'm not condoning it, it's just, what are you gonna do?

Some residents were in fact very clear about the value that they place on diversity relative to other social issues in the community. This created a very real tension for residents who struggled to reconcile these values, as Franklin, of Edgewater, laments:

You know, it's just gosh, it would be so much easier if we just went out to the suburbs. And her brother lives in [a northern suburb], and they've got a nice park district system, and they've got a nice pool that they can go to, and they've got a huge back yard, you know, where the city lots you don't have much outdoor space. So it's constantly in the back of our minds, you know, if we're doing the right thing, if we made the right decisions, if life could be easier.

Amidst that, there is the hope that their investment in their community and in their property will pay off. Lucy, of Edgewater, said:

Gentrification was just starting. And, you know, uh, it was perfectly all right with me. Yes, I know what's happening in the neighborhood, and that's why I want to live here. Uh, I want to live with gentrification. I want to live with the yuppies. And yes, the neighborhood is going gay. Hallelujah!

The level of commitment that was given to sustaining racial diversity amidst other social forces is perhaps best illustrated by the forms of community action, which as chapter 2 revealed were by and large not devoted to justice or sustaining diversity. Recall that most efforts were instead geared toward fighting crime, getting to know one's neighbors (oftentimes to help subvert crime), contesting development decisions, and beautification efforts. While all such efforts are important in any community, and here undertaken by residents who most often do place at least an abstracted value on their communities as diverse spaces, the social action and racial ambivalence continues to recreate a comfortable white habitus rather than a community that has the economic and social benchmarks, such as quality public schools or housing safety nets, to make for diverse governance and empowerment.

WHITE HABITUS IN A DIVERSE COMMUNITY

The strategy in this chapter has been to analyze the links between color-blind ideologies and community action using the racial formations theory. I claim that a coherent racial project takes place in the linking of these ideologies with individualized and collective action in these neighborhoods. Because the dominant ideology does not allow for a coherent and utilitarian approach to analyzing and acting around the significance of race in these communities, community members are left to act on the only means available to them—individualized, consumption-driven actions and those that keep the community safe and intact for the interests of whites and homeowners.

Where Hartmann and Bell (2007) have shown the gap between discourse and action in their analysis of happy talk, given their national sampling methods there is no way to link this to individual or community action, especially as it takes place in definite local contexts. Here I have done just that. Further, where Bonilla-Silva and others have shown the influence of color-blind ideologies on racial attitudes and responses to national policies and hypothetical scenarios, here we see the ways individuals immersed in a concrete local setting are influenced by these ideologies. Far from the back stage, overt racism and discrimination that Picca and Feagin (2007) identify, here well-meaning residents who are already committed to their communities through their social action and community organizations grapple for meaning and attempt, but ultimately fail, to connect those ideologies with meaningful social action.

These are people who do like the diversity in their community, wish there was a wider representation among the leaders in the community, hope that their communities are wise investments and viable places to live, and yet cannot or do not connect that desire to collective social action that would counter the market forces that could unravel them. Just on the contrary, consumption and the marketplace remain the easiest and most comfortable ways to both do diversity, as evidenced in their individualized actions, and to enhance and promote the community, as evidenced by the range of collective action taken.

This racial project, these links in the chain between ideology, discourse, individualized, and collective action, work together to produce and reproduce white habitus. That racial project is articulated in figure 4.1. White habitus itself is the engine of color-blind ideologies, as the

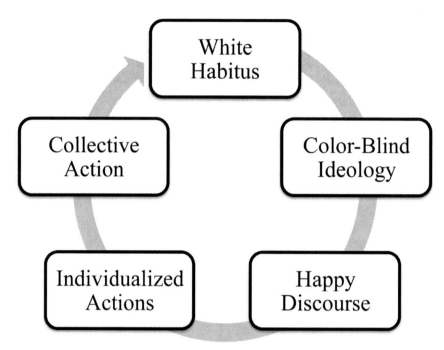

Figure 4.1. Reproduction of White Habitus

ideology of color-blindness explicitly legitimates and leaves intact the racial order that it purports to explain. Those color-blind ideologies then inform the discourse, which is explicitly coherent to a race-positive and yet empty set of principles. Because that discourse itself is contingent on a white normative center, individualized actions will seek to add to rather than alter that white center by consuming diversity instead of engaging it in community or democracy. Further, collective action, the end result of either discrete individual market choices (including the real estate market) or as a collective enterprise, will seek to protect this white center in its sensibilities, safety, and security (economic and otherwise). As such, it then reproduces this white habitus, even in a racially diverse environment. This cycle continues until it is consciously disrupted, something vitally needed in these communities if their diversity is to be maintained. Whereas with Bonilla-Silva (2003) we have "Racism without Racists," and in Margaret Andersen (1999) "diversity without oppression," here we have white habitus in a racially diverse community.

Yet before turning to solutions, which as this chapter and the previous indicate must include disrupting these color-blind ideologies and intentionally including diversity as a key community initiative, we will look deeply into the self, to consider how the whites who are overrepresented in these communities see themselves in racial terms, and in relation to that diversity. Despite the white habitus that typically leaves whiteness and color-blind ideologies unchecked, I argue that whites are still negotiating their relationship to a diverse community, and in that process their own racial identities, in ways that are more complex than typically recognized in the academic literature. More fully understanding how they see themselves is critical to supporting their efforts to improve their communities and, hopefully, more fully develop their efforts to sustain its racial diversity for the benefit of all.

5

CONTEXTUALIZING WHITE IDENTITY

This book begins like a satellite, locating a still-rare stably racially diverse community, zooming in to discover its contours, its history, its geography, who lives there, and who becomes active in shaping its policies and dynamics. Chapter 3 began broadly by looking at the reach of color-blind ideologies and their still-strong influence in a community that embraces not only its diversity but also its liberal, and perhaps even progressive, identity. Chapter 4 looked even more carefully at the discourse around diversity, and how it unintentionally re-created a white habitus, a white-centered environment, within these diverse communities. This chapter, finally, continues that zoomed-in lens and looks at what it means for whites to consider their own racial identity in this community.

Whites get my focus in this chapter in part because they constitute the majority of active residents and the participants whose voices have been appearing in this book. But as Matthew, of Rogers Park, notes, they also hold disproportionate power:

> In Rogers Park is that there is a group of, I would be willing to bet, no more than 200 people that represents 80 percent of the leadership in the neighborhood. And that's CAPS people, the block club people, the non-profit organization people, people at the university. . . . And within that

200 people, I'm going to guess that probably 80 percent of those folks are white, middle class professionals . . .

And so you're really missing an entire—200 people representing a neighborhood of 65,000, when two-thirds of the neighborhood is minority, and you don't have hardly any representations. We have almost no Spanish speaking leadership. I mean, zero. You go to community meetings, there's never translations in Spanish. It almost never happens. The biggest thing you get from people is "We made a flyer in Spanish."

As Matthew's comments reveal, the opportunity to examine how whites situate their own racial identity is often just as rare as the stably racially diverse communities I'm studying. Part of my argument is that this environment provokes consideration of whites' racial identities in ways that homogenous communities do not. That said, the recreation of a white habitus, detailed in chapter 4, still makes this a difficult enterprise. Not all active residents are as racially conscious and critical of power relations in the community as Matthew. However, I argue that most residents are in some manner or another conscious of, and acting in relation to, their white identity. This negotiation of a white habitus and a white self inside a racially diverse community provides space to examine the complex role of white racial identity in the contemporary United States.

WHITENESS STUDIES

While the sociologist W. E. B. DuBois was writing about whiteness as far back as 1920, for most of our history, scholars have failed to study and theorize privilege to the same extent that we have studied disadvantage. This changed radically in the 1990s, when historians, legal scholars, sociologists, psychologists, and those in the humanities began to place whiteness under academic scrutiny. This enterprise has not been without its critics, some of whom assert that "Whiteness studies are constructed on a foundation that consists of broad generalizations, ontological and epistemological claims, normative and evaluative statements, prescriptive advice, political goals, and critique—supported by histories, biographies, stories, anecdotes, recollections, and ruminations" (Niemonen 2010, 62).

The reality is that the vast majority of whites have lived lives of extreme segregation (Massey & Denton 1993), and as a social group are recipients of an often unexamined racial privilege. As Bonilla-Silva and Embrick note, ". . . whites have very little contact with blacks in neighborhoods . . . [and] do not interpret their isolation from blacks as a problem because they do not interpret it as a racial phenomenon" (2007, 330). They argue that a white habitus creates a wall over which many whites cannot climb in order to develop meaningful relationships with people of color. As I also demonstrated in chapter 4, they claim that "whites' extreme racial isolation from blacks does not provide a fertile soil upon which primary interracial associations can flourish regardless of blacks' level of assimilation" (2007, 341).

Further, as this book has revealed, the ideologies mandating color-blindness are so strong, and racial privilege for whites so often invisible (McIntosh 2005), there is an undeniable lack of awareness about the reality of continued racism among the vast majority of the United States population. Prior research has demonstrated that it is common for whites to deny that they are racial subjects, that is to say, that whites even have a race (Lewis 2004). Perhaps on this basis, some race scholarship has assumed rather than discovered an absence of white racial identity, to the detriment of a more complex understanding of contemporary racism and inequality. Bonilla-Silva, Goar, and Embrick claim: "Though whites hardly think of themselves as possessing a racial identity, current research suggests that white identity becomes salient when white dominance is challenged" (2006, 232).

While their claim likely would hold true in most settings, to convey this as a universal fact limits rather than enhances our understanding of both white identity and contemporary race relations. This conceptual and methodological error is a classic example of research that does not take our daily lives as grounds for exploration, but rather assumes categories and meanings that sorts lived experiences into those conceptual molds (see D. Smith 1990). Such practices are, in effect, ideology rather than sociology. As Charles Gallagher asserts,

If whiteness is treated as a monolithic identity based on privilege or the assumption that all whites harbor certain negative (or positive) attitudes toward other racial groups, researchers will miss the opportunity to examine the social complexities and the social geography of how and where racial identities are constructed and the multiplicity of meanings that define whiteness (2000, 213).

It is from this realization that leading scholars in the field are calling for work in this area—"the systematic empirically grounded gathering and telling of white people's narrative about their understanding of their race, as opposed to the way whites define the racial 'other'" (Gallagher 2000, 214; see also Lewis 2004).

This enterprise is not without its challenges. Ideologies like color-blindness are, after all, structured to maintain privileges for dominant groups. This recognition goes as far back as Marx, who famously claimed in *The German Ideology*, "The ideas of the ruling class are in every epoch the ruling ideas." Nevertheless, as Lewis says, "Empirical research on whiteness . . . has the potential not only to push the boundaries of our understandings about the role of whites as racial actors but also to extend our understandings of how race works more generally" (2004, 637). Gallagher makes a related point, saying, "The view that 'Whites' consciousness of whiteness is predominantly uncon-sciousness of whiteness' or that 'Transparency, the tendency of Whites to remain blind to the racialized aspects of that identity, is omnipres-ent' is no longer a sustainable narrative in the wake of racial identity politics" (2000, 215).

Scholars have also encouraged researchers to push beyond studies that see whiteness as only cultural, and thus divorced from the very real, material workings of power from which whites systematically benefit (M. Anderson 2003). Instead, the scholarship itself must be dynamic: "In order for whiteness to be demystified and stripped to its political essence, our interviews must generate counter-narratives of whiteness . . . " (Gallagher 2000, 203). It must explore the complexities of white racial identity in ways that preserve white agency and the diversity of white standpoints while still casting a critical eye toward the role of institutionalized white privilege, from which whites cannot individually divorce themselves.

With some important exceptions (Lewis 2003, Myers 2005, Perry 2001, Zaijek 2002, Eichstedt 2001, Hartmann, Gerteis, & Croll 2009, Hughey 2010), white racial identity is otherwise absent from racial iden-

tity research in sociology, which is striking given that whites still constitute roughly 72 percent of the U.S. population. Further, Paul Croll has
found that roughly 74 percent of whites place some importance on their
racial identity, and uses survey research to "explore the relationship between American ideals and white racial identity and the duality of strong
white racial identity held for both progressive and defensive reasons"
(2007, 613). He argues that white identity seems strongest at either end
of the political spectrum, producing something of a U-shaped curve as
views move from conservative to progressive political values. Clearly it
is time to move beyond the question of if whites are conscious of our
racial identities and begin to explore the complex and nuanced question
of how that identity works. Racially diverse communities, as this chapter will demonstrate, provide an ideal place to examine this question,
as they are also places where one's racial identity will be salient in the
years to come.

TOWARD AN EMPIRICAL EXAMINATION
OF WHITES IN THE EVERYDAY

Whiteness studies is currently evolving to consider "the nuanced and
locally specific ways in which whiteness as a form of power is defined,
deployed, performed, policed, and reinvented" (Twine & Gallagher
2008, 5). This new trend in research has largely broken from static,
essentialized accounts of white identity, yet still at times implies that
whites are always working to maintain their supremacy. When that happens, scholars miss an opportunity to learn about the nuances and complexities of racial identity for whites, which contexts like a diverse community can reveal. As previous chapters have shown, the whites in this
book are in most cases not acting out of racial animosity, and, despite
the pitfalls I examine in chapters 3 and 4, are indeed quite supportive
of diversity initiatives. Many are also, as you've read, critical of racism
and continued segregation in these communities. Given the number
of whites actively involved in these communities, this book is in large
part the story of whites struggling to make meaning of their support for
diversity, their involvement in racially diverse neighborhoods, and their
attempt to move beyond color-blindness.

As Twine and Gallagher note in their assessment of recent literature, new research in whiteness "is characterized by an interest in the cultural practices and discursive strategies employed by whites as they struggle to recuperate, reconstitute, and restore white identities and the supremacy of whiteness in post-apartheid, post-industrial, post-imperial, post-Civil Rights" era (2008, 13). While white privilege has indeed remained intact, such a reading of literature runs the risk of assuming that whites are acting with the intent to maintain racism and their own racial supremacy rather than acting in response to a diverse social context that supports diversity and, as this book examines, an ambivalence and uncertainty about how to speak and act in relation to it. When we shift our lens accordingly, we find a complex, dynamic, contested social system in which we can all exert influence.

It should be noted that this critique of some of the new terrain in whiteness studies is not meant to be a defense of white privilege or the whites who do work actively to maintain supremacy in particular social environments. A rich literature exists that documents those dynamics. Instead, I assert that there remains a need for researchers to take seriously the grounds upon which whites are actually operating in their daily lives. As Lewis asserts,

> Studying whiteness or white people absent of social context obscures the precise reason why it is important to focus on whiteness in the first place—in order to remove the cloak of normality and universality that helps to secure continuing racial privilege for whites. . . . It is important to do so, though, not because it is hip, not because whites have been left out, but because doing so is a necessary step in confronting the continuing reality of racial inequality (2004, 642).

For example, Kathleen Blee's (1991) research on women in the Ku Klux Klan, while certainly critical of the KKK and their support of severe and often violent forms of racism, is most interested in tracing the complexity of how those women understand their worlds and seek empowerment therein, which, given that empathy, can allow for counter-framing and forming antiracist social movements that can capture their concerns. So far in the bulk of the new research in whiteness studies, most researchers are still missing the context and nuances which tell us how race actually operates among whites, and the diversity of thought, action, and experience among whites. Croll's (2007) U-shaped model is a positive start, but much more work needs to be done.

This recognition is one of the central reasons I developed an interest in studying diverse communities and their active members. Following Eichstedt (2001), in this chapter I argue that whites who are active in diverse communities must navigate a "problematic white identity." That is, whites who are active in racially diverse communities must somehow reconcile their whiteness with their community context. I made the choice early in this study not to directly ask residents about their racial identity. I instead allowed these discussions to emerge either from the participants themselves or in relationship to other discussions of diversity and community issues. As such, it is perhaps not surprising that I got only a small number of direct articulations about white racial identity. At the same time, I believe that those that did emerge are highly significant for their unprovoked character. They are articulating this meaning because it is vivid for them. Further, in many cases, responses to my questions about housing choices and community involvement are themselves indicative of a white racial identity that *is* being mobilized, even if not in direct terms. In the following sections I explore both direct manifestations in the context where they emerged, and the indirect manifestations of white racial identity that were active in relation to race and diversity in these communities.

DIRECT ARTICULATIONS OF WHITE IDENTITY

Like most conversations, the ones I had with people in this book did not begin with "As a white person," or "Because I am white . . ." This is in part due to the normative nature of whiteness, its ability to go unrecognized in most settings, and in part because I chose to allow self-examination of whiteness to be revealed by the participants themselves, rather than asking them to stumble through an answer that asks, "How do you think of yourself as a white person in this community?" For that reason, most of the 41 people in this book did not make statements like the ones above. However, when it came to the particular contexts of crime, diversity, or political organizing, some did. In none of the above three contexts could their white identity be taken for granted, and in some cases their privilege as whites could not go unnoticed. In the words of Eichstedt (2001), their racial identity in some way became "problematic." As such, discussions of crime, of diversity in the neighborhood, and political organizing became a catalyst for residents to consider and articulate their own white identity. The discussions below demonstrate the reality that whites are capable of reflection about their racial position in concrete local settings, and the complex challenges associated with acknowledging whiteness, or breaking from the color-blind norms.

Crime and White Identity

While crime issues in the neighborhood heightened whites' awareness of their racial identity, it did necessarily not do so in ways that were defensive. Kurt demonstrates an awareness of the protection that his white skin gives him in the neighborhood, even in the context of active crime:

> I remember walking across the street one day in a light rain, and I noticed an officer. . . . I stopped and I said, if I can ask you a question, I said I live in this building here and I know that you're using it as a police lookout. I said I'm wondering what it is I need to be watchful of in this neighborhood, are there any known issues?
>
> And he looked me up and down for a good 20, 30 seconds. . . . And he says, "Well, frankly, sir, I don't think you have anything to worry about." And I gave him this kind of cockeyed look, and he says, "Well, I mean, our drug dealers and our gangbangers, they don't look like you." True story.
>
> And I said oh, okay. So I kind of took that to mean that, you know what, I'm probably looking a little upscale beyond the folks that are around me.

While his analysis of "looking a little more upscale" may not be the same one offered by a social scientist, his talk is not laden with fear or racial venom. Instead, it more closely mirrored the measured, educated stance that residents took when discussing issues of crime more broadly, as detailed in chapter 3. It's merely an emerging awareness of the social context for his white skin, one that is likely to continue to develop over time.

The same carefully considered evaluation of local crime issues was revealed in Todd's discussion of a period in the early 2000s when Rogers Park experienced a spurt of development:

> I'd venture to say a large chunk of people were displaced outside of the community entirely. It created a lot of tension. I'm guessing, but this is just sort of an observation that there was probably more petty crime, more assault and battery between people who were not related since then than ever before. I'm not saying people didn't get knocked over the head and their money stolen before, because they did and they always will, regardless. But a lot more I will say—and this isn't just, you know, white guy, middle-aged white guy speaking, this is, you know, black friends of mine who will tell you that there's a lot more aggression on the streets.

Todd's explanation does not overstate the impact of the crime or contain reactionary discourse about its inception. Again it reflects the measured contemplation of these matters that were discussed in chapter 3. Further, during our conversation, in a room where one white person was speaking to another, Todd engaged his racial identity explicitly, at the same time contextualizing it relative to "black friends" who agree with him to racially neutralize his position as nonreactionary or racially defensive.

Todd's explanation is complex, both hinging on his white racial identity and seeking a race-neutral foundation for his explanation. After all, the "black friends" narrative is a common refrain for neutralizing race-focused discussions, and recall that Todd in other places stumbled around the question of racial integration in his friendship networks. But that does not mean that his analysis is incorrect. Indeed, his observations could be empirically tested. He maintains race-neutrality without abandoning a critical examination of his own white identity. His further comments about this issue reveal an even deeper reflection on his racial identity as it relates to his community:

> *Todd:*—and for the most part I'm seeing [that aggression] from younger kids. Mostly black kids, um, who now, like never before, see me as sort of the man. As the white yuppie living in Rogers Park. And they know nothing about me. They don't know that I've lived here for 20 years and that I make very little money, that I don't see them as anything other than a

human being walking down the street. . . . I'm talking about, you know, waiting for a stoplight and, you know, getting lip from some kid for no reason because you're a white guy sitting in a new car waiting for the light to change . . .

MAB: And how do you manage that? Do you say something?

Todd: I don't think it changes the way I think over time. I guess I come from the school of always trying to understand where that person's coming from. Hell, part of me says, "Well," you know, "to them I'm a privileged white guy who's run this world for, you know, 100 years or so." You know. I guess I get it to some degree, you know, I understand where that comes from, but fall short of trying to make some sort of blanket statement about *black* people and the way they see *white* people.

Note in this passage how his white identity remains direct, as does his frank discussion of racial dynamics, even while he becomes increasingly ambivalent and defensive about the situation he described. On the one hand, he resents "getting lip from some kid for no reason"—reasons that fail, he argues, due to his income, his tenure in the neighborhood, and even his color-blindness, as demonstrated in his assertion that he "doesn't see them as anything other than a human walking down the street." At the same time, he is thoughtful about what he believes to be true about the kid's life, and places himself squarely within the power structure that his white race and male gender reflect. And he does so immediately before returning to a comparative if not somewhat resentful look at how whites may be stereotyped by blacks and vice versa.

Another white male Rogers Park resident, Mitch, also spoke about some of the ways in which blacks and whites in the community encounter and perceive each other:

Mitch: [There is] this really adversarial relationship with the kids—the black youth and the cops, and so, you know, a lot of the black youth have this really kind of antagonistic attitude towards not only cops, but a lot of times white people. I mean, I've had them, you know, spitting on the sidewalk behind me, or things like that. Saying something.

MAB: Like what kind of things would they say?

Mitch: Uh, there was one time [my friend and I]—were walking, and they made—I can't remember specifically, but they just made some remark trying to provoke us, and we just walk and ignore it.

While less explicit than Todd in his own personal feelings about this encounter, Mitch's description of these events does hinge on his own racial awareness and the times when that has directly impacted him in the community. In the scope of that interview, Mitch never showed any of the ambivalence or resentment that Todd had displayed about his encounter above. Yet both men reacted to such a setting with an articulated awareness of their racial identity and its significance in that context.

Diverse Communities and White Identity

The context of a racially diverse community was itself another catalyst for white racial identity to be articulated. As Charles Gallagher notes: "Contemporary racial politics and the effect of the media have made it practically impossible for many whites not to think about themselves as occupying a racial category" (1995, 300). In the following passage Erin had been reflecting on her work experience in Rogers Park, which is itself linked to the neighborhood's diversity:

> You know, I'm kind of always aware that we're sort of dealing with completely radically different cultures and races and backgrounds. I can't really, I'm having trouble calling a specific example. In fact most of the time I find that because of my position as a white person working with people of color, there's benefits in terms of kind of bridging the gap in terms of people's perhaps biases or ideas or discriminatory attitudes about [people]. Um, those are times I think of it being beneficial.

Much like the white women in Eichstedt's (2001) study of antiracist activists, for Erin her white skin became an energizing rather than a restrictive identity, as she claims it in order to bridge racial gaps and educate other whites. She is saying that because of her close interaction with people of color in her workplace and neighborhood, she is able to serve as an ambassador of sorts to other whites to help them overcome their ignorance or racism. This not only excavates her own racial identity, but marks it as one distinct from other whites whom she is telling me she is unlike and thus able to serve. This was in fact also a common indirect way white identity was articulated among interviewees, as I explore in-depth in a later section of this chapter.

The context of diversity in Edgewater was also used as a platform for articulating Evelyn's white racial identity, in particular her feelings of comfort in such an environment.

> *Evelyn:* We used to think that we were the perfect community because the population was something like 20 percent black, 20 percent Hispanic, 10 percent other, Asian and 50 percent white. And going back to when I was in school, one of the fellows for the Board of Education, I forget what his title was, but he dealt with demographics. And he talked about tipping points. And so the reason I said that, to me, that was kind of a perfect proportion was that, although the whites are 50 percent, I liked that because I was white. And that the other populations were balanced and in significant enough numbers so that they would not be discriminated against basically . . .
>
> *MAB:* And when you say "because you're white," that means?
>
> *Evelyn:* Well, I think there's a comfortable feeling. I mean, I'm being very realistic.

This actually became a somewhat awkward moment in the interview. Evelyn worked to make scientific or objective her feelings about a desirable racial mix within a community, relying on experts to make a claim that was not necessarily racist. At the same time, her claim was emphatically one of feelings. She likes the community because she is white, and she can live in a comfortable environment for whites that she hoped would also eradicate discrimination for nonwhites. When I asked the follow-up question about this feeling, she emphasized the role of comfort for her as a white person, and then seemed to cut away from a need to be scientific or objective, but rather emphatically "realistic."

Indeed, the contact hypothesis measures this exact phenomenon, arguing that intergroup contact is one of the most effective ways to reduce prejudice. While further research has shown that the dynamics are somewhat more complex than mere contact, requiring a number of other stipulations and working differently for differently positioned groups, the premise and the promise is there. In fact, it has shaped much of the research around neighborhood integration and segregation (Krysan 2002; Emerson et al 2002; Yancey 1999; Farley & Frey 1994). Ellen, in her passage above, is being honest about what's comfortable, and for her that is directly linked to her racial identity. This comfort is important to her in a diverse community. She is the resident who in another place in our conversation said that her dream is walking to Lake Michigan without having to look behind her shoulder, particularly as she travels the two to three blocks within the Winthrop-Kenmore corridor. There too, her white racial awareness is activated. While she does not say "because I'm white I feel unsafe," the context on which that statement is hinged does that same work. Whether direct as in the passage above or indirect in her other comfort statements, it is clear that the context of a diverse community works as a catalyst for her white racial identity to become salient. To use Zaijek's (2003) term, it invokes a "problematic white identity." Note that "problematic" does not mean "bad" or even something that would create "a problem." Rather, it means that something gains complexity and significance, and must be reconciled in a particular social context.

Political Organizing and White Identity

A further catalyst for white identity awareness was political action within these diverse communities. While not occurring in Rogers Park or even Chicago, the following excerpt details one resident's campaign work for Barack Obama. Doing this work, Fred invokes his own racial identity, which he later links back to his experiences within Rogers Park:

> And I have knocked on doors in [other states], and I realized white people were coming to the door, and they were looking at the button, they were looking at me, and I realized they were listening to what I had to say, they agreed with what I had to say. I don't think they really knew how to believe in the message coming from an African American. Like, they had never done that before. They were studying me to figure out, well, here's a guy who looks like me, a blue collar. . . . "This guy looks like me"—and I can kinda shift my demeanor to fit the situation. And they were studying that. And I realized they've never seen this before. They've never seen guys that look like me come to their door and pitch for a "blackie." That's how *they're* looking at it.
>
> The other thing I noticed was, knocking on doors at black houses, the whole family would gather at the door to hear the pitch. And I realized, all right, look, 90 percent of these people are with us already. Why are they

listening to me so carefully? And it was the exact same thing. They'd never seen a white guy make a pitch for a black guy before.

Here, unlike in the passages above, it did not take actual diversity to invoke Fred's white racial awareness, for he was doing campaign work in segregated communities outside of Chicago. Instead, the mere association with one black person—even if that person did go on to become the president of the United States—became the diverse association that invoked his white racial identity. He felt studied and intensely scrutinized by both blacks and whites for his willingness to support not only a black man, but a black man who he believes will be understood in racist terms by those whites, given his use of the term "blackie." He also assumed that they didn't know how to hear Obama's message from Obama himself, or from anyone other than a white person. He thus also produces a discourse on whiteness at the same time that he articulates his own white identity.

Further, he engaged in code-switching among these other whites. Code-switching is precisely the "switching of demeanor to fit a situation" that Fred explained to me in his interview. Previous studies of code-switching have explored how nonwhites navigate racial terrain in the United States (see E. Anderson 2000). Fred provides evidence that whites also code-switch. As Fred's case reveals, whites who code-switch are doing so precisely because of an awareness of how their own racial identity will be perceived in a social context. Like any code-switchers, whites may also make adjustments to their affect, language, and demeanor according to their shifting environment.

I was interested to hear more about how this worked back in Rogers Park, given what he told me about his political involvement in the community:

> *MAB:* And I'm just wondering, when you mentioned this idea of this white guy pitching for a black guy, did you ever have an awareness of being, in the local campaign, a white guy pitching for [Rogers Park's] diversity?
>
> *Fred:* Oh, absolutely. . . . Race affects everything, yes. Yes, absolutely. Absolutely. I mean, it just depends on the situation. One of the more challenging environments to walk into is the Hispanic community, because there's a language barrier first. I don't speak Spanish. You're expected to

be respectful in a way that other communities might not expect it. You're an official. You're supposed to wear a suit. You're supposed to be clean-cut, you know, very polite, all that.

However, in this neighborhood, a white guy that walks in a suit usually wants something. He might work for the government. You know, it's not a good encounter. So we could say, "Hey, I'm not here—I don't want anything," you know.

And people would often write checks. "No, no, no, no, no. Don't give us any money. We're just here—I just want to say hello." And you'd see the shock on their face, like, "Oh, hello." You know, kinda look at each other, and then they'd say something to each other in Spanish. "Are these fuckin' Gringos crazy?" You know, it's like "what are they doing here?," you know? "What do they really want?"

In this instance Fred's code switching involves cleaning up and wearing a suit, and conducting oneself with deference and dignity in response to what he feels he understands about his correspondents' culture. He exhibits acute awareness of his own racial position in that process, and also an awareness of how he may be read in racial terms. Later, he also talked about this process when in interaction with other racial communities, namely the need for whites and blacks to self-define issues in political campaigns and how he shifted his strategy with different groups as a result.

While certainly the interactions above are complex for their assumptions around culture and values, they are not interactions where the participants felt threatened or challenged based on their race. Yet those challenges did occur in the context of political work, as evident in the passage below, where Shannon discussed the politics within her building:

Shannon: . . . Sometimes there's an issue over this being previously a . . . less white people living in the building and now more white people, and someone like me coming in, and trying to get an association in better order, then there was definitely distrust with that and why I would need to have control over things. And I wasn't really trying to control them, I was just trying to get the structure in place that should have been there, so that even if I wasn't involved, it would still be there.

MAB: Right.

Shannon: So there were definitely some conversations about that, me, that kind of thing.

MAB: And how did those conversations play out?

Shannon: It was really hard at first. . . . Um, definitely one person on the board was really direct and said, "Maybe you have a hard time with a pow- erful black woman like myself." That was said to me directly. . . . I decided to just share that with everyone next time I was in a public venue and say, "That's a racist comment. For you to say that is racist. And I'm not racist, and I didn't appreciate it. And if you think it's OK to say things like that I think you need to examine where you're coming from, because I'm not comfortable with you saying things like that to me. Because I'm not racist in that way. And I'm working hard not to be racist in any way." You know, I just tried to have an open conversation about it, and she was pretty un- happy with me for a little while, but actually now she and I are pretty close in a way, we work together on a lot of efforts in the neighborhood now. . . . She just, I think she really had had some probably bad experiences with people before. And her expectation was that I was trying to control everyone because I didn't think they had any capabilities.

Shannon still seemed affected by that experience as she retold this story, and showed a certain level of discomfort not only with the situ- ation itself, but also in her retelling of it in specifically racial terms. As such, both her retelling of the story as well as the incident itself emerge as highly self-racialized for Shannon. She had, through this challenge, become acutely aware of how she was being perceived as a young white woman coming into the community, seeking to make changes. Her in- teraction with the black woman in her story took an overtly racial turn, and she had to defend her actions and beliefs in direct response to both her racial identity and how that was being read in her political context. While it is arguable that the woman's critiques of Shannon are quite valid, despite Shannon's dismissal of them as "racist," this awareness would only further deepen the level at which she is making sense of her own white racial identity.

It is clear in all of these interactions that in the context of diverse communities, there were many catalysts for white identity awareness. It also became clear to me in the course of this project that whites were not only engaging their racial identity in direct terms, but also in indirect terms via conversations about other issues. That is, even when not direct, that engagement was still taking place. Discourses around diversity and race themselves are a form of identity construction for whites, particularly in the context of diverse communities. They show us how they think about their race not overtly but by proxy of other contexts and issues. That identity construction is explored in the following section.

INDIRECT ARTICULATIONS OF WHITE IDENTITY

While the instances above demonstrate that the participants in this study are indeed aware of their white racial identity and how it relates to their social context, there were other responses that, while not articulated directly, were of necessity predicated on the respondents' awareness of their white racial identities. This included, for some, even discussing their role in a racially diverse community. Paul Croll's (2007) conception of a U-shaped curve related to a strong white racial identity is again instructive in this regard. One of Croll's index measures is how alike his participants believed they are to others in their racial category when it came to prejudice. He notes, "High scores . . . indicate strong symbolic boundaries based in whites' ideas about cultural membership" (2007, 621–22). That is, whites who believe they are different from other whites will exhibit a stronger white racial identity. That element of Croll's research is verified by the indirect manifestations of white racial identity in this section, where whites make a distinction between themselves and other whites.

Given their context of living in and becoming involved in a diverse community, it is significant that white participants most often constructed their racial identities in opposition to hegemonic notions of whiteness. Black, Latino, and Asian participants, on the other hand, did less racial identity construction, instead emphasizing a racially diverse context as vital for their protection. Because whites don't need this protection in a society that grants whites racial privilege, whites worked to expand diversity beyond the scope of race, and emphasize nonracial aspects of their identity as a means of belonging.

Casting Diversity's Wide Net

In chapter 4, I explored the ways that diversity's happy talk involved an expansive definition of diversity, which worked to uphold the white habitus of the community through whites' extraracial emphases. I provided some examples, and argued that despite the fact that it is specifically *racial* diversity that defines the community, many residents created a color-blind notion of diversity in order to buy into the community's diversity. Here I use that foundation to argue that this same process, which I illustrate with additional examples, must also depend on whites' awareness of their own racial position. This self-awareness of one's own whiteness provokes the speaker to emphasize other aspects of one's identity in order to legitimate their claim to a diverse community. Thus, while the emphasis of the discussion is on anything but race, the centrality of race in diversity discourse is maintained. Whites are aware of this, and strategically navigate around it.

If that were not the case, there would be no need for the expansion of this net. After all, most of the residents of color that I interviewed were explicit about the value of *racial* diversity in their own connection to the community. They rarely made the efforts to emphasize the extraracial components of the diverse community. Whites, by contrast, are often weary of owning their whiteness and uncertain about the stakes that they may hold within the valuing of racial diversity. Prior research in whiteness studies has already told us this much. But that does not mean that they are unaware of the presence and the salience of their racial identity.

For example, Tom's list became very detailed with respect to ethnicity rather than race as he discussed the diversity in Uptown:

> There are a lot of *very* poor people here, there's a lot of *extremely* rich people here, and everything in between. There's Romanians, Russian Orthodox Jews, you name it, this part, even our little part of Uptown has it. Hispanic, Laotian, Vietnamese, Chinese, Romanian, Russian Jews, gays, straight, old, young, kids in strollers.

Similarly, Kurt, in Uptown, described his building as follows:

> We had everything under the sun. We had European, Baltic nations, Mediterranean nations, African, Canadian, Vietnamese, Cambodian, Thai—I mean, we had literally the world living.

Children made the list in Uptown for Hank:

> Eh, first of all, it's a very diverse community. We have different nationalities. We have people from different countries, and we have different, eh, age people here. A lot of children in this area.

Age was also celebrated *as* diversity in these neighborhoods, particularly in Rogers Park, which has an infrastructure that facilitates more contact among renters and owners than Edgewater, with its single family homes, and Uptown, with its micro-communities. Wendy said:

> And by the way, that's one of the wonderful things about Rogers Park, too, that it's not just that I really have friends of all ages here. . . . And I think there's something that happens in Rogers Park that sort of evens out the age. When we got married, we had people from the community of all ages and it was just really fun, you know, to have this diverse group of people there. It really was.

While again it's factually correct that diversity embodies more than race, to emphasize age or equate diversity with age, as Wendy does here, is a significant distinction for a white person to make.

Shannon had the most exhaustive list among those I heard:

> Um, but there is *so* much, it's—there's *so* much diversity in Rogers Park, it can be overwhelming sometimes, so in our *building*, you know, some of the issues and some of the diversity would be just people have such different opinions, you know, their *age*, their economic background, race, religion, I mean our building alone is just one of everything.

This "one of everything" discourse is another instance of consuming diversity individually, in appreciating the benefit it has for a person rather than for a community. But it is also a mechanism for whites to deflate, while still including, the place that their own whiteness holds in the community. I don't mean to imply, in my analysis of the meaning of this maneuver, that racial diversity is the "correct" way to value diversity—but rather to see this expansion as a racial project among whites linked to their ambivalence and uncertainty in relating to matters of race. I argue that it hinges upon it. In the next section I further argue that this list-making is vital in whites' ability to form a meaningful relationship to a diverse community.

Opting In by Opting Out

Despite the ambivalence around race described above, almost all of the whites in this study mentioned, without prompting, their appreciation for the racial diversity in these communities and their desire to see it maintained. The last section explored how whites navigate a racial core of diversity in part by stretching the boundaries of "diversity" quite far beyond race. This section explores how many whites, equating diversity with disadvantage, also work to emphasize the aspects of their identity that are disadvantaged rather than privileged. In short, they "opt in" to their place in a racially diverse community by partially "opting out" of their racially privileged identity.

Many, like Shannon, did this by discussing age, an identity that at various points in the life course has associated stereotypes and disadvantages:

> Age tension in our condo for example, all the time, you know, between the owners and the people that have lived there 17 years and those who are new and want to change all this stuff and do all these things. And you're like "Is this the ignorance of youth?" or is it "You're set in your ways?," or I don't know which way it is.

While naming a very real conflict in her building and in her struggle to form relationships with others in her community, she emphasizes one way that she has experienced marginalization—as someone who perhaps embodies "the ignorance of youth." Here she is not only talking about the frustrations stemming from that experience, but also speaking about diversity broadly, giving an example of how that diversity can cause problems that are not related to race.

The emphasis on non-privileged aspects of one's identity is often, of course, itself a political move. This is particularly vivid when gays and lesbians in these three communities talk about the appeal of living in a diverse community, as Tom does here:

> Because we moved up there because, in a lot of ways, we really liked the diversity of it. I mean, of course I'm gay. You tend to want to be in a diverse place so you don't stick out, so that's part of it.

The need for a safe space among subjugated groups is of vital importance (see Lorde 1992, Tatum 2003). The point is not to criticize those like Tom for emphasizing that need, but rather to notice the choices related to self-definition for whites in a racialized context like a diverse community. With respect to white identity, it would be too easy to say that Tom and others like him are proving their lack of racial awareness. Some previous scholars of whiteness have made that leap. Instead, I argue that we need to at least appreciate how this choice is at least structured, in part, on recognition of one's racial identity. Race is being negotiated for whites relative to the social setting, and noticing these dynamics will tell us more about the complexity of race and racial privilege in the United States.

The specific equation of diversity and disadvantage provides a ripe context for this dynamic to be revealed. As discussed in other parts of this book, whites are aware that diversity is often equated with race. As such, their stretching of diversity's boundaries is centered around their ambivalence in claiming a piece of that diversity as whites. There also seems to be a strong implication that diversity is not merely about difference—diversity instead is understood as something relevant only to those who are disadvantaged. Diversity means people of color, women, the disabled, the elderly, youth, gays and lesbians, the working class, immigrants, and not whites, men, the able bodied, middle-aged, middle-class, heterosexuals, citizens, etc. Their personal connection to diversity in these communities is not through owning their privileged racial category, but instead through emphasizing an element of their personal social disadvantage.

Gays and lesbians were not the only whites who identified this way. Laurie, of Rogers Park, connects it to issues with her body, that in turn propels her to struggle for racial justice:

> I—almost all my life—have struggled with weight issues. And so [I] was very often the butt of childhood jokes, and harassing and that type of thing. And so I think that growing up with that type of issue, whereas some people might not have that as much, has always led me to really closely relate to any group of people that may struggle more in making their way in society, I would say.

This empathy on the basis of one's own personal disadvantage has long been identified as a fertile source of coalitions in the struggle for social justice (Hill Collins 2000). Laurie is someone who retains those justice-focused grounds, as other aspects of our conversation suggest. She spoke clearly and passionately about racial justice in the community and in the United States. For most others, however, this connection was less clear.

While any relationship to diversity is valid, and arguably those directly linked to social justice the most fruitful for sustaining it, the impetus to relate to diversity in nonracial terms among whites is important to notice. It reifies whiteness as something unmarked, nonracial, and therefore thought to be "invalid" in a diverse space. This is despite the reality that diversity is not just a smattering of disadvantage. Indeed, for these neighborhoods to thrive, community must be extended between whites and people of color, homeowners and renters, and citizens and immigrants. This trend of equating diversity with disadvantage, and emphasizing one's own disadvantage to stake a "legitimate" claim to a diverse community, also speaks to the uneasiness with which whites may directly engage their whiteness—and as such robs whites of meaningful ways to directly engage our own racial position and thereby democratize its placement within structures of power.

"Other" Stories

A further way that white identity emerged indirectly was through stories. From a social scientific perspective, stories always have a purpose, and as such are vital for communicating meaning and sharing histories. They are more than mere entertainment. Stories become familiar within a culture; they communicate a shared history. They are also used to supplement and validate arguments (Bonilla-Silva 2003). When a story is told to me as a researcher, it is far from a digression, but rather a direct linkage to other stories, other people, and often shared meaning. Over the course of this study, I became familiar with neighborhood events and issues through the stories people told me. Residents in these communities told stories about interactions with other neighbors, about growing up in other locations, about challenges to power, and about significant community events. Each story told carried with it an implicit story about who each participant is, usually via who they are not. Their stories revealed how they think, how they interact, and how they understand their social world and their place in it.

Eduardo Bonilla-Silva's examination of story lines and testimonies is a central piece of his work in *Racism without Racists* (2003). There he distinguishes between story lines—vague and yet familiar discourses which take up a particular position, and testimonies—more direct and often less easily disputable stories in which the teller is a central character to the story. Each is significant for Bonilla-Silva, as each is meant to convey a particular position: "Through stories we present and represent ourselves and others" (2003, 75). Story lines and testimonies stand in for forthright opinion, and can be used to back up and validate an uneasy position. Both play a key role in discourse, as ideas are crafted around events in order to communicate ideologies and meanings.

In this section I analyze what could otherwise have been dismissed as "digressions" in my interviews—semi-extended stories specific to events they either witnessed or participated in, which were told in response to my open-ended questions. Residents in Edgewater, Rogers Park, and Uptown used story lines and testimonies in various ways: to illustrate their appreciation for diversity, to disrupt the political correctness which they felt was eluding important issues, to reveal and critique racism in their communities, and in some cases, to reveal their own racial ambivalence.

Othering Other Whites

One central theme in the stories told among residents in these communities was criticism of other whites who exhibit racism. In the passage that follows, Patty and I had been talking about the racially tolerant character of Rogers Park and those who did not choose to remain in that environment. In that context, she discussed a program, which was common several decades ago, where white families hosted black children into their homes:

Patty: We had Operation Hospitality here, where we had some kids bussed in from Oakwood on the South Side. And I had a little girl that came to my house for lunch every day. From the South Side. And then she made her confirmation here, we had her family to our house, and you know, had an after-confirmation party with a cake, and you know, all the refreshments, and they didn't have a car. So then my husband drove them all home to the South Side.

So this wasn't an issue for us, but there were people who looked me right in the eye and said, "Well, *I* wouldn't do that." And those people moved. And they moved out *far*. They got as far away as they could . . .

MAB: Do you remember what your response was to her, when she said that to you?

Patty: . . .Um, I don't. I don't know whether I bothered to defend it . . . You know, . . . there are some people, you know, it's a mentality. Some people have it, some people don't. . . . And there were others that, you know, "I wouldn't do that. I couldn't do that."

Um. . . . And somehow it was never a surprise. You sort of know the people who would react that way, and you know the people who won't react that way. And mostly the people who would react that way were not my friends, because they weren't people that I felt that I had all that much in common with.

In this story the event and its details are less important to Patty than the distinction she is making between herself as someone who would host a black family in her home and others who would not. She is constructing her identity as a tolerant white person as well as the kind of white person who would resist white flight and its associated homogeneity. Note, however, that neither Patty nor many of the other voices in this section actually challenged their racist counterpart. Instead, Patty and others reveal to me, and likely others to whom they tell these stories, that they are someone who embraces her diverse community.

Others resisted this white flight and homogeneity by critiquing people from their past, most often family members. Wendy and I had been talking about her desire to know people from different backgrounds, and I asked her how that became so important for her:

I'm very interested in different cultures. I think it maybe had part to do with the fact that I grew up feeling sort of different than people around me. . . . I grew up in a fairly liberal household—my father was one of the most liberal people in town and yet he was really a liberal more by talking than by really experience, you know. And I saw how he would condescend to the black people in his life. And I personally just really needed to get beyond that and, you know, just look at people as people. You know, I really needed to do that. But it wasn't something that happened overnight. It was something that had to be worked on, you know, for me, anyway.

Wendy and other whites talked candidly about the process of dealing with diversity, the hurdles to clear, the work involved. It is something they are actively seeking—something they are choosing to consume, or at least actively constructing as a choice. And more often than not, they are doing so in opposition to other whites and other, non-diverse places. Such thinking depends on a binary, as do all Othering practices (de Beauvoir 1989 [1953]). If a white person presents herself as a tolerant, and perhaps also progressive person, she is doing so in opposition to the Other whites who uphold racism. In that process, as Croll's (2007) model also indicates, she is articulating her white racial identity.

Laurie's comment exemplify this process. She told me the following story when explaining why matters of race were important to her. The interracial relationships in her past were of vital importance to her personally, in her appreciation for diverse communities, and in her very intentional choice to move to Chicago with the hopes of encountering like-minded people. She told me a story about her work environment that still upset her today:

And my two managers, the ones that ran my company, were open and outright racist bigots. . . . And they would say stuff all the time about every different racial and ethnic group that came in. . .

And my last straw there was—I was responsible for [some hiring]. . . . And it's real challenging to hire people for positions like that. And so I was having really good luck with it, but I guess I was hiring too many black people for their liking, because they called me into their office and said that they didn't want me hiring any more black people . . .

I felt sick to my stomach. I went out in the hallway after this conversation and I was just, like, shaking. . . . I had the chills. And I was just like, I cannot believe what I've just been told by someone in this day and age, you know . . .

This story marked Laurie's stance on issues of bigotry and racism, affirmed her belief in the reality of racism, and also draw a distinction between herself and other whites who hold these views. By telling me about other whites, she constructed a racial identity as a different kind of white person. Gallagher has noted that in particular contexts, ". . . recognition of whiteness is not solely a reactionary response to challenges from nonwhites; it is also a reflection of the need to provide oneself with a narrative of whiteness that does not demonize white as a racial category" (1995, 300–1).

Stories about bigoted whites were not the only ones scrutinized by the white residents in this book. Several were active in criticizing other whites or liberals in the neighborhood, putting the politics that they might wear on their sleeves in the context of their other choices and actions. Todd had been discussing the character of Rogers Park as a liberal, diverse place, and said:

> *Todd:* But . . . I know a lot of people . . . that have lived here a long time that are not terribly liberal. That don't vote. Um, that are not so accommodating to other people. . . . It's not that I'm trying to say that these people are racists or that these people are . . . seething bigots walking around, but, you know, they're sort of more anti-establishment libertarians who don't want to be shot and have a little bit more fear than the average person walking around in Rogers Park, hence all the *guns* that I've seen.
>
> I was astounded the first time. Sitting [a local café], [several] years ago, I ended up in the middle of this conversation with all of these people who I would've never in a million years thought—and out of about a dozen people sitting outside, and these are people I would see every day walking across the street. The one thing that was similar is most all of them were over 40 and maybe even 45, most of them men, most of them white, but there was a few women thrown in, um—out of about a dozen people I think there was 9 people who said they either had a handgun on them at that time, or owned one.
>
> *MAB:* Wow.
>
> *Todd:* And I just scratched my head in disbelief. And my only question was "Why?" You know?
>
> *MAB:* Did you ask that question?
>
> *Todd:* Oh yeah, and the answer was simply, you know, "There's all these thugs running around, you know, I gotta be able to protect myself."

Todd was aghast even in the retelling of a story that had happened a number of years ago. His story revealed both the underlying fear and coded racism among other whites with professed liberal values in Rogers Park, and also showed me that he is not someone who adheres to such reactionary beliefs of practices.

Wendy, whose passage about her father I shared earlier, also told me this story, on a very similar theme, about an unnamed political figure in the neighborhood and an interaction she witnessed between him and some young black teens:

> *Wendy:* I won't tell you who the person is. But . . . one day, I was walking down the street and next to me was walking a young black boy. He must have been maybe 9 or 10 years old. And he was going to the Science Academy. And he, you know—I could tell he was just kind of a quiet, really well mannered young man.
>
> And I saw three white guys who lived in the places that they owned on the block, one of them who became a candidate, chasing a bunch of black teenagers down the street and holding baseball bats and swearing at them. And this young boy was watching this. And I could see the fear in him. And he said to me, "Why are those men chasing those kids down the street?" I said to him, "That's really not OK that they're doing that." You know. "They really shouldn't be doing that."
>
> And I went and talked to the man the next day. I said, "You know what, that was really not OK that you did that. This is what happened. This young boy saw you doing that. And I don't care what those kids did. It's really not OK to do that."
>
> *MAB:* What did he say?
>
> *Wendy:* What he said to me is, "Well, I wasn't carrying a baseball bat. And I know who the other two were and they probably shouldn't have done that," you know. And then he said something about how the kids were making a lot of noise in front of the house and jumping on a car and whatever. OK. They were teenagers. They were doing something they shouldn't have done. OK. Probably. Um, but it was boys and girls and it wasn't like they were doing something violent. They weren't selling drugs. They didn't have guns on them. You know what I'm saying.
>
> So, no, he really didn't—he was kind of quiet about it. He kind of shook his head. But, you know, that stuck in my mind. It did. I thought, well, if he feels like that, how does he feel about the rest of the neighborhood?

In this story the image of Rogers Park as some place where diversity is uniformly celebrated is undermined. In telling the story, Wendy showed me her objection to such behavior and her willingness to challenge another white person who would chase black teens down the street with a baseball bat. She also revealed her doubt about this political candidate's racial politics in a diverse community. Much like Todd's story above, this event had stuck with her and deeply bothered her, and in the retelling she became quite affected. It is clear that not only telling this story, but also her choice to intervene, has a relationship to the type of white person she has chosen to be, an identity construction that also is consistent with other points in our discussion.

The following story, told to me by Mitch, another Rogers Park resident, works similarly in its critique of local business owners and police. We had been discussing people's reluctance to patronize some local businesses, and he mentioned a Mexican restaurant right near an el stop:

> I go in there all the time, and the cops are always coming by and shooing the kids away. And some of them may be in gangs, and some of them aren't. Some are dealing drugs, some aren't. But they all get lumped into the same category. Doesn't matter. I'll be sitting in there eating with friends, and these black youth will come in and order something, and the guy is like chasing them out.
>
> There was one time the one kid came in and he was ordering, and he had his friend in, and the guy said, "Well, you can stay, but your friend has to leave, because I'm not going to let anyone stay in here who's not ordering anything." So then the cops came in, and . . . asked if you want this guy to leave, and he said yes, and those guys are always kind of sitting and watching out the door to see who's out in front.
>
> And it's the same with [another restaurant]. There was one time [a friend] and I were walking by after seeing a movie, and we were coming back to the [train], and all the sudden there's like six squad cars, and a bunch of kids with their hands on the hoods, and we go into [that restaurant] because he wanted to get something to eat on his way, and (laughs uncomfortably) there's like 10 kids sitting in [there] to stay clear of the cops. So it's just kind of a weird situation there.

Mitch is critical of racial profiling among police and business owners in the community. While he did not intervene in the situation, he articulated his perception of racial profiling as a common practice as well as something he does not support. In so doing, he makes a distinction about what kind of white person he is, juxtaposing himself with those who believe it is necessary to harass young black men in his community. It should be noted that the police officers and business owners are not themselves exclusively white. This is all the more indicative that he is telling me something about himself as a white person just as much, if not more than, telling me something about racial dynamics in the neighborhood.

Other instances of this juxtaposition have already been analyzed in other chapters of this book, such as John's discussion about a community meeting where he feared that his neighbors sounded racist, or Matthew's assessment of the CAPS flyer he saw in Rogers Park. In that process, these residents delineate themselves from whites whom they perceive to be racist. They challenge the racial undertones present in these mostly- or all-white community meetings. Their stories about these particular challenges are not only stories about the community issues we were discussing, but also about how they construct their racial identities as whites. Far from race-blind entirely, or homogenous in their thinking, many whites are quite cognizant of race and its significance both in the community and for themselves in it. This is despite the fact that their racial identity is not directly being articulated.

For example, several residents spoke candidly about some of the racial undertones that had been mobilized in what had been the most recent aldermanic campaigns. This was the same campaign that Wendy discussed above. Fred was talking about the diversity in Rogers Park, and quickly turned his attention to those who specifically use racism to undermine it.

> Um, so that was really at the core of the whole campaign, was that, you know, we have economic diversity, we have racial diversity. Tremendous racial diversity. Probably the most racially diverse zip code in America. Um, but in order for that to continue, you know, we can't have. . . . Even Bobby Kennedy once said that most white people want to do the right thing, but it's hard to get people to do the right thing if they're scared.
>
> And the other side of the aldermanic election was this guy, who masterfully played on those fears. . . . It was very ugly. It was a lot of code words. On one of the flyers they famously sent out was a girl that kinda looked like you, but a few years younger, with a bag over her shoulders. So just this terribly frightened little white girl, kind of a *Birth of the Nation* kinda

thing, you know. [She] was looking behind her, scared, saying, "Do you feel safe in the 49th Ward?" with a little black shape, black shadows, in the background.

Fred's critiques were only about one white person, the aldermanic candidate who used such a poster in his campaign. But by proxy, he is also critical of the white demographic he felt was its target, one who he argues is prevented from doing the right thing because of their racial fears. He invokes Kennedy to back his assertion and constructs a racial identity for himself as a progressive, rather than one of the whites who would succumb to such fears.

He then told an additional story to validate his assessment of the racial imagery in the poster:

> I held this flyer up for this roomful of union guys, who were from places like the South Side and Jefferson Park, and they knew right away what they were seeing, you know, "Whoo-whoo," you know. And it was interesting, because these were people that wouldn't live with people of color necessarily in their own communities. They wouldn't raise their kids with people who don't look like them. But they recognized right away what this was, and just how ugly it was. And that kinda struck me as evidence that perhaps something a lot of us are taking for granted in terms of general progressive values locally didn't really exist in quite as widespread a fashion as we had all kinda thought. Um, and it was a real wake-up call, frankly.

In this story, Fred not only extended the distinction he makes between himself and a subset of whites in his community, but also to yet another group of whites from which he also demarcates himself—working-class whites who would *not* live in an integrated environment. He shows how even *they* were able to recognize the racist undertones that the candidate was using to mobilize whites in Rogers Park, a well-known integrated community. The layers of whiteness being deployed here are manifold, and in these layers Fred situated himself not only in opposition to racist images and codes, but also to several other groups of whites with whom he refused to identify. He sees himself, his story emphasizes, as a different shade of white.

This process at times came in the form of direct challenges to other whites, as discussed by Erin from Rogers Park:

We have a neighbor who takes a real ownership of the building and the neighborhood and he tends a lot of people's yards. And when the crime was happening, he was just completely racially profiling, and telling people, "Oh, it was a *black* guy, and he looked like this" and really hadn't seen him at all. And so I guess I'm kind of comfortable confronting those things and saying like, ". . .You know, I just want to be really careful, you know. We don't want people to start . . ." So I think I, you know, confronted him in that way. "Are you sure you saw him?" and "Yeah, it was a black guy, it was a black guy."

While the details in her story can't be verified—the race of the criminal or whether or not her neighbor had in fact seen him—her story is also a story about herself, both in her opposition to racial profiling as well as in opposition to the white person who was, she emphasizes to me, so adamant that the crime spree was linked to black residents in the neighborhood. She is not the kind of white person who fears her black neighbors, who will jump to race-based conclusions in the crime spree. She is also not the kind of white person who will leave such remarks by other whites unchecked. She is not saying "I am thinking about my white identity" directly, but her remarks are centered around this same process.

The matter of Othering other whites is delicate. Certainly it is in part another iteration of the familiar story line established by Bonilla-Silva, where "respondents insert these testimonies as if they were expecting absolution from listeners about the possibility of being regarded as racist" (2003, 92). But, consistent with my critique of some strains in whiteness studies, I think we miss some complexity around racial identity and how people in real settings contend with issues of race if we stop our analysis there. Yes, these whites are strategically positioning themselves as someone who is not racist in this discourse. However, they are also always articulating a racial identity in that process. While in situations like these it is certainly possible that one strategy is to say, in essence, "Please don't think I am a racist!," most of these comments reveal instead a commitment to either diversity broadly or antiracism specifically. They are stories about a white racial self and a story about race in these communities, always in the context of their displeasure with the community's racial politics or racist realities. Were I to hold these up as yet another example of whites preserving the racist status quo, that complexity, and those multiple realities, would be lost. The same is true when whites Other other places.

Othering Other Places

Many whites in these communities drew a distinction between the kind of environment in which they were reared and the kind of environment they have chosen as adults. Such a distinction created a binary between their environment of origin and their current diverse communities. Fred was responding to a question I had asked about where he'd lived prior to Rogers Park. After naming the community on Chicago's South Side, he went on:

> I can sum up for you the racial environment there by telling you a very short story of the South Side Irish Parade in 1983. Standing on the roof of a bar with a bunch of people, and the crowd was cheering for this Bernie Epton guy, who was running for mayor as a Republican against Harold Washington. And, you know, all these people are cheering for him, and one of them said, "He's a fuckin' Jew," you know. And the other one just looked at him and said, "Yeah, but better a Jew than a nigger any day."
>
> And that, really, I couldn't sum up the racial environment on the South Side better than that little snippet of conversation. That's exactly how the entire community down there pretty much related to each other.
>
> It wasn't just white racism. It was black racism on the other side of the equation, and it was consistent. It was reliable in that sense. You could count on it, if you walked on the wrong street, being chased off of that street, whether you were white or whether you were black. And it was a very, very, kind of a depressing place to be in if you had any kind of progressive values at all, and so . . .

I had not asked Fred to sum up the racial environment of his youth—merely where he had grown up. While he knew that I was interested in race and diversity in my study, he used this story to also tell me something about the overt nature of racism in his past environment, as well as where he landed politically. It is also notable that this happened very early in our interview. I went on to ask him if he was someone who identified with progressive values, and he answered, "Yeah, you could say that" with a smile and a laugh, as though this were an understatement. In doing so, he self-identified as an antiracist white, a progressive, and someone who is happier in a liberal, diverse community like Rogers Park than on the South Side.

This distinction was common among the whites in this book who grew up in homogenous, and in their view constrictive, environments. Erin had been discussing how she wanted to be connected to those who were not like her, and said:

> . . . and part of that, I think, is also coming from [another Midwestern city], which is *so* white bred. I mean, I never knew anyone. . . . I think there was one African American girl who went to my high school, but it's not only being *Caucasian*, but I came from a *Catholic* upbringing. I never even knew anyone of even another faith tradition until I left [home] and went to college. So I was really looking for something really different than that.

Like Fred, Erin's white identity is complex in that her discussion of likeness is centered around a homogenous white Christian norm. She names that homogeneity and decouples herself from it in her current residential choices. She wants to move beyond that "white bred" environment, and she has. In articulating that process she is indirectly articulating her racial identity. She is white, and yet delineating herself from whites in homogenous, and as she implies, somewhat narrow environments.

Dan was responding to a question I asked about his attraction to Edgewater, which he had emphasized as a very appealing place to live:

> I was raised in a suburb of [a Midwestern city] where a Catholic person was an interesting difference. It was culturally barren. And . . . I just found it to be stifling and bland, lacking of flavor and interest. And so Edgewater area is enormously diverse, enormously. And so it kind of has a great sort of representation of the cultural richness of Chicago. Chicago, that's such a huge appeal for the city itself, is that diversity, and with all the different festivals . . .

Dan's definition of this city's suburbs as barren, bland, and lacking "flavor and interest" is congruent with common stereotypes of white culture and communities (see Myers 2005). This is certainly a piece of the desire to consume diversity that I explored in chapter 4. Yet it is also a way for Dan to construct his racial identity in opposition to the homogeneity and blandness he associates with white culture.

The same sentiment is echoed here by Angela, who was answering my standard question about where she'd lived before moving to Edgewater:

> Well I grew up in, uh, on a farm outside of [a Small Town], [in an Upper Plains State], so I would describe it as being fairly socially isolated, and small farm kind of community. Small town. And my first three years of high school was at sort of a regular, not a real big Catholic girls school, and then that school closed my junior year and so had to finish at the public high school. . . . And there was minimal diversity there. In high school I think there was one Native American girl that was in our class, and then in the town there was a small Native American population and these one small family group, like two or three brothers who were African American. And I was interested in that as well and had a little bit of exposure.

Angela paints a vivid picture of the isolation of her upbringing, and stated it as an impetus to seek diversity in her adult life. In so doing, she constructs the places as binaries to one another, and herself as one who has, instead, chosen diversity.

WHITES AND DIVERSE COMMUNITIES

I emphasize the binaries that are central to this discourse because they are central to the practice of Othering. Like all processes of Othering, they were enacted to show me who they *are* just as much as who they are *not*. If hegemonic whiteness is about being bland, boring, and stifling, then these residents are not only distancing themselves from this racial association. They are also distancing themselves from an understanding of whiteness with which they find personal dissonance. Even if they are not explicitly telling me how they think about being white, they are telling me something about an alternative kind of whiteness, one that can appreciate diversity and which is not at home in a homogenous environment. Certainly this appreciation is not without its problems, as detailed in chapters 3 and 4. Yet what our emphasis on problems so often misses is the very real fact that people are reconciling their agency and their sense of identity while they face those problems.

All of the stories I've explored above serve a dual function. They tell me something relatively unpleasant about the racial dynamics in communities, be they their communities of origin or the racially diverse communities in which they now live. Yet they also construct an alternative white identity. Their criticism of other whites is, after all, predicated on their own racial self-concept. Although they are not directly saying to me "This is what my white identity looks like and this is how I define it," they are showing me how it operates in their recognition of racism or intolerance in other whites and the choices they have consciously made in reaction to those whites. They are telling me, in essence, "I am not *that* kind of white person."

While it may seem counterintuitive to devote so much attention to whites in the context of a diverse community, their overrepresentation among community leadership as well as the site itself provide fodder for some meaningful conclusions. Centrally, these communities serve as a site for a "problematic white identity"—that is, a space where whiteness cannot be simply assumed or taken for granted as it can in so many other segregated contexts. I assert that this site allows for an expansion of white racial identity research—one that can account for not only the catalysts and representations of such identities directly, but also for the indirect articulations of this identity which are based on residents' own assertions about whiteness and diversity. It may also indicate that as the racial diversity of the nation grows, there will be fewer spaces where the white norm is unchecked. As more whites own and reconcile their white identity with their changing local communities, there is as much opportunity for dialogue and democracy as there is for repression. Beginning to notice these early articulations, direct and otherwise, is a first critical step toward moving beyond color-blindness and toward that democratic ideal.

Specifically, this chapter advances our understanding of whiteness by demonstrating everyday sorts of instances where whites are aware of their own white identity, and speaking and acting in relation to it. This happens in direct settings where contexts of crime, diversity, and political organizing do not allow their white identity to go unnoticed; their awareness of their racial privilege is also acknowledged and articulated in those same settings. Their code-switching, rarely if ever previously examined among privileged groups, is evidence of this negotiation.

Further, I argue that there are many more indirect settings, also quite common to everyday life, where whites' talk and action is predicated on their racial self-awareness, even if it is not explicitly stated. While whites are often weary of directly discussing race, their own or others' in these settings, some previous studies have taken this as evidence of racial oblivion or defensiveness. I argue that both logically and in relation to other points of evidence, weariness is not evidence of ignorance. It is likely yet another outcome of our color-blind ideological system, where we know the significance of the color line in our lives and communities but do not learn ways to meaningfully discuss or act around it.

As the new research in whiteness studies moves forward, studies like this one will continue to reveal the myriad ways that whiteness is understood and deployed relative to the social conditions in which it is embedded. This research also allows for an inroad toward better understanding the complexities, contradictions, and variety of dynamics upon which race and discourse is deployed in these communities, something that survey research alone often cannot capture. It is my hope that the depth of understanding of self-concept, ideology, discourse, choice, and community action that this book has traced provide a needed glimpse into the preservation of these communities as diverse places, and inroads for making them not just racially diverse but also socially just. Chapter 6 explores just those challenges and possibilities.

6

THE PATH AHEAD

Sociologist Elijah Anderson's newest book, *The Cosmopolitan Canopy*, provides an ethnographic account of several urban public spaces, "settings that offer a respite from the lingering tensions of urban life and an opportunity for diverse peoples to come together" (2011, xiv). He argues that this emphasis on civility and tolerance are part of a cosmopolitan experience where visitors "discover people who are strangers to them, not just as individuals but also as representatives of groups they 'know' only in the abstract," arguing that canopies can provide a "profoundly humanizing experience" (2011, 276). Anderson invests great hope in the enjoyment that people from most walks of life find in the cosmopolitan canopy, evidence that acceptance and peaceful coexistence are possible in the contemporary United States.

At the same time, his book reveals what he also calls fault lines or cracks in the canopy, times when blacks and other people of color are reminded of whites' assumed entitlement to public spaces like restaurants, and also their racialized fears. Anderson holds this up as a realistic and yet hopeful picture, something that can be held alongside the normative civility without fundamentally disrupting the cosmopolitan space. I think that my work in this book goes deeper into the dynamics of racially diverse urban spaces. By systematically interviewing those who have actively shaped these diverse urban neighborhoods, and ex-amining in-depth their racial ambivalence, racial identity, and thinking around diversity, I am able to explore the whiteness of contemporary diversity politics, and also the ways that diverse communities can move beyond the superficiality of the canopy, or the happy talk, to make these communities just and sustainable for all.

First, to be clear, Anderson is studying specific public places, and not neighborhoods. In Edgewater, Rogers Park, and Uptown, the public beaches are clearly the canopies, along with some very small business districts along Broadway in Edgewater, the theater district in Uptown, and perhaps streets like Morse or Devon in Rogers Park. However, these are the same zones that I critiqued as places of genuine interracial contact and interaction, or as alone equivalent to the practice of nurtur-ing diversity. To consume diversity, to individualize the connection to it and remain at the superficial level of chit-chat and food, is not likely to offset the market forces that could gentrify these communities and push working-class residents, many of whom are people of color, out. In de-scribing canopies, Anderson notes, "They need not interact intimately. . . . They give one another the 'aura' described by Georg Simmel, al-lowing each person to swim about in this sea of diversity while being largely left alone. They come, interact in a broad sense, obtain what they want, and return to the world outside this setting" (2011, 51). While it is encouraging to hear about the enjoyment of diverse public spaces from middle-class people and whites, this alone will not create or sustain just, diverse, democratic communities.

Fundamentally, this is because most of the active residents I inter-viewed for this book are no more able than anyone else in the United States to discuss issues of race in anything other than color-blind terms. Living in a diverse community, enjoying and celebrating that diversity, identifying with liberal or progressive politics, stumping for Obama, or shopping and eating from immigrant communities does not mean that one develops a race cognizance, the ability to navigate outside of the very narrow confines of color-blindness that have dominated the politi-cal discourse in the United States in the post-Civil Rights era. And it is these realities, taken in tandem, which have thus far created racially diverse communities that reproduce rather than democratize a white habitus, white wealth, and white privileges inside of otherwise diverse spaces. After all, as Anderson notes, "in navigating the quasi-public spaces here, there is little sense of obligation to the next person other than common courtesy" (2011, 275). Courtesy has never alone brought racial justice.

Indeed, what my methods reveal that Anderson's observation of canopies does not is the deeply seated ambivalence around diversity and matters that are perceived racially in these communities. While there is celebration of diversity, gay white homeowners are embraced more readily than working-class Latinos, and all residents are looking after their individual financial well-being and the education of their (sometimes hypothetical) children first and foremost. While this is to be expected among people in the United States from all walks of life, there is a stark absence of community efforts that are seeking to maintain the diversity of the community as a stated objective, or to support access to quality education for all children in the community.

A close look at the public schools in these communities is instructive in this regard. As tables 6.1–6.3 will show, the school with the lowest percent low income among the three neighborhoods was a selective naval academy, where the percent low income was 82.1 percent. This school shares a building and campus with the larger high school, where the percent low income is 95.7 percent. The schools are also disproportionately black and Latino. The tables below, using data available from the Chicago Public Schools website, only reports the top two racial categories in each school. Whites are in that category, always in second place, only twice among the 22 schools.

Table 6.1.   Rogers Park Public Schools

School	Level	% low income	% Black	% Hispanic	% Asian	% White
Passages	K–7	84.9	54		22	
Swift	K–8	90.5	39	31		
Pierce	K–8	84.3	11	70		
Hayt	K–8	92.4		46	22	
Goudy	K–8	95.6		28	42	
Senn	9–12	95.7	38	43		
Rickover Naval	9–12	82.1	21	62		
		avg 90.7				

Source: Chicago Public Schools

Table 6.2. Edgewater Public Schools

School	Level	% low income	% Black	% Hispanic	% Asian	% White
Passages	K–7	84.9	54		22	
Swift	K–8	90.5	39	31		
Pierce	K–8	84.3	11	70		
Hayt	K–8	92.4		46	22	
Goudy	K–8	95.6		28	42	
Senn	9–12	95.7	38	43		
Rickover Naval	9–12	82.1	21	62		
		avg 90.7				

Source: Chicago Public Schools

As discussed in chapter 2, whites consistently use race as a proxy for "good" schools (Johnson & Shapiro 2003), and low-income schools are also often synonymous for poor quality. Residents told me that there had been a schooling committee in the Edgewater Community Council at one point, but at the time of my research it was defunct. The mismatch between the demographics of the neighborhoods, their schools, and the activity of active residents is stark and revealing. The need for quality and equal schooling for all, regardless of race or income, is clear. Were there a concerted effort to embrace and elevate these schools, were they to reflect the racial and class diversity of the community, were schools not a factor in residential choices, the benefits for communities and the country would be dramatic. To date, we are still waiting on those changes.

After reading this book, I hope it is more clear why that may be, even among a group of well-intentioned, hardworking, deeply committed individuals who do indeed celebrate and care about the diversity in

Table 6.3. Uptown Public Schools

School	Level	% low income	% Black	% Hispanic	% Asian	% White
Goudy	K–8	95.6		28	42	
McKutcheon	K–8	98.4	61		22	
McPherson	K–8	87.2		76		13.6
Stewart	K–8	98.8	54	36		
Stockton	K–8	93.5	50	39		
Trumbull	K–8	91.9	16	60		
Uplift	9–12	96.2	81	12		
Lake View	9–12	88		60		14
		avg 93.7				

Source: Chicago Public Schools

their communities. First, I demonstrated how strongly the color-blind ideologies that permeate our entire nation have still taken hold in these communities. While they take on a specific liberal flair, the active residents shaping these communities are still not often able to talk or think outside of the color-blind mandate. When they attempt to do so, they either rely on familiar racial codes, or lapse into incoherence. I do argue that these codes and incoherence are not alone evidence of deep-seated racism. In a racialized social system, we are all impacted by the dominant way of understanding the world; this is a system that still produces racial inequality. However, my analysis of how this ideological system works in a diverse urban community known for its liberal or progressive politics reveals more complexity and more desire for change than prior studies, often undertaken in more homogenous settings.

Further, recall that while the pitfalls of color-blind ideology are still very much present in these communities, their racial diversity is still celebrated and embraced. Despite that, I demonstrated how a white habitus is still the foundation for, and the driving engine of, the discourse and social action in these communities. While prior studies have demonstrated the "happy talk" surrounding diversity generally, in this concrete setting where action around diversity is so vital, priorities are usually given to individual choices and consumption-based practices. Whereas Anderson would celebrate these as canopies that indeed may make people more tolerant of diversity generally, as the tables earlier in this chapter demonstrate, this commitment does not reach such vital places as the public schools or other institutions which would create racial justice.

Without this commitment, all we may be left with are some of the presentations of self that I detailed in chapter 5, where we superficially enjoy diversity and construct a public "cosmopolitan" self but do not think or act self-critically or democratically to achieve racial justice. This does not mean, however, that the whites in these communities are either racist or unaware of their racial identities and privileges. First, as I always tell my students, deciding who is racist and who is not is not a very useful exercise. After all, we are all members of a deeply racialized society, one that creates advantages for whites to the detriment of people of color. Labeling individuals as racist or not does nothing to help us see and struggle to change that system. More critically, I demonstrated that whites often are thinking actively about our racial identities. This happens directly when the setting of a diverse community will not allow residents' whiteness to go unexamined. But it also happens indirectly in many other kinds of settings, settings not necessarily exclusive to racially diverse communities. While many whites remain weary of discussing or acting around race, they are often not racially unaware. They simply lack the language, education, or opportunities to engage more deeply and critically with their racial selves.

PROGRESS AND HOPE

As hopeless as that may sound, I fundamentally share Anderson's view, "That people find such pleasure in diversity is a positive sign of the possibilities of urban life in the twenty-first century" (2011, 282). In fact, I find that pleasure vital. Without it, key venues of support for racially diverse communities and the democratization and social justice that I think they must entail are academic, esoteric, and unlikely to move people to change. Like Anderson, I find evidence of that pleasure and that civility throughout the interviews with the 41 people who shared their views and their work with me for this book. I see this happening in three key ways.

First, everyone I interviewed saw diversity as an asset for the community. It is something that people want and that people enjoy. This is evident in the white racial identity constructions that I explored in the last chapter, in the happy discourse around diversity (which, remember, is genuine even while it is thin and glossy), and in the consumption patterns that take it in, both viscerally and literally. Most everyone I interviewed was living here intentionally, at least for the time being, and thus represent thousands of people who are at least willing to live in a diverse community without the clear goal of gentrification. There has been no promise that these communities will gentrify, that the rent gap will open wide enough for entrepreneurial investors to flood the market and create profits. Thousands of people are living there anyway.

Second, connected to that pride, residents in this book care deeply about their communities. They are working hard to keep them stable economically, to support local businesses, and to keep their streets and parks and beaches clean and safe. It is tremendously inspiring to interview people who have so little time and energy left to give, and yet tirelessly devote it to planting a new garden, cleaning up the beach, attending zoning meetings, meeting with their alderman, serving as a court advocate, or any number of such endeavors that I heard so much about during these interviews. The 41 people I interviewed here, and the others with whom I could not connect, represent a commitment to work to further improve the diverse communities to which they are already committed by residence. Their attitudes around diversity and community would mean nothing without their work and their efforts.

Finally, despite a disproportionate amount of white homeowners, everyone wanted to see a more diverse and democratic representation among its active residents. Some residents simply bemused this reality, but others were quite articulate in their criticisms of the community dynamics that have made it that way. Several are beginning those hard conversations about race, pushing community accountability not just to the hip new bars in the theater district or to the police monitoring "teens" on their block, but to the community more holistically. And yet the challenges that I've identified in this book persist. So what is to be done?

SUPPORTING AND BUILDING DIVERSE COMMUNITIES

Working to support or build diverse communities will take work on many levels, national and local, personal and policy-driven, ideological and economic. The following sections draw heavily on some key sources that have written more extensively than I do here about what does work, and what is needed to support and sustain diverse communities. With the political and economic environment constantly in flux, and the United States' ambivalence about race, racial inequality, and social justice so deeply-seated, it could be argued that "the only way through it is through it." After all, that's what this in-depth look at these communities has sought to do. People are experimenting, at times trying to reconcile competing values, and aside from devoting themselves to their communities in a myriad of ways, also trying to have personal and professional lives. That said, if there is one theme that is important, it is that we must keep talking about race, and we must be intentional about our desire to support the diversity that we appreciate. That is not easy in a nation structured by color-blindness, but in the famous words of Justice Blackmun, "In order to get beyond racism, we must first take account of race. There is no other way."

National Level Recommendations

Fundamentally, it is vital that we find a way to have a broader and bolder conversation about racial inequality in the United States. Eric Holder, the U.S. Attorney General under President Obama, recently stated: "Though this nation has proudly thought of itself as an ethnic melting pot, in things racial we have always been and I believe continue to be, in too many ways, essentially a nation of cowards" (Holder 2009). He went on to comment, "And yet, if we are to make progress in this area we must feel comfortable enough with one another, and tolerant enough of each other, to have frank conversations about the racial matters that continue to divide us" (Holder 2009).

His comments were met with outrage in much of the mainstream press. But all social psychological and sociological evidence suggests he is right. This book demonstrates that even though they take on a localized, liberal form, the national pressure to stifle frank discussions of race, and the color-blind push to minimize the significance of race and racism, remains strong. This is despite these communities' rare identity as both racially diverse and overtly liberal. If communities such as these still cannot fully break from the color-blind mandate that is continually reproduced in our popular media and within our political discourse, then it will be increasingly difficult to nurture and sustain racial diversity, and more significantly racial justice, in our communities.

These color-blind ideologies have not just blocked our ability to talk honestly and directly about racial realities in our nation. They have also greatly constricted our ability to discuss and nurture diversity. While today the term has largely been reduced to the generalized but positive "happy talk" that prior national studies have examined, and this book probed in-depth in a concrete environment, the diversity discourse has deep political origins in social justice movements. Those movements sought not only to appreciate diversity but also to connect it to our personal and formal politics. If even in these liberal, diverse communities, where residents have chosen and embraced such diversity, we are still blocked from meaningful discourse around race and an overt racial justice or even pro-diversity agenda, there is all the more reason to challenge this discourse of "diversity without oppression" (M. Andersen 1999) at the national level. Electing a black president is not sufficient to achieve racial justice or even racial harmony, as the reaction to Holder's statement and the deeply racialized contention around Obama's relatively moderate presidency confirms. Nurturing and supporting diverse communities at the national level will only be more difficult if this stranglehold on frank discussions of race continues.

Significantly, prior scholarship has consistently suggested that advocating for racially diverse communities at the national and federal level is key (Ellen 2000; Nyden et al 1998; Maly 2006). While seemingly basic, pitching for both the existence of, and positive features within, diverse communities plays a vital role in calming either overtly racial or "race-based neighborhood" (Ellen 2000) fears about these communities and their financial stability. Direct marketing, positive national media attention, political stumping, and affirmative marketing programs not only help to underline the legitimacy and success of such communities, but may also play a role in attracting stable businesses and jobs to the area, which in turn elevates the legitimacy of such communities and their economic stability.

Ellen suggests that modest governmental intervention, including at the federal level, is also justified in these communities (Ellen 2000). She argues that such intervention has both an economic and a moral legitimacy that most Americans could accept. Primarily she suggests the kinds of information campaigns detailed above, but also tax-based incentives for people to move into these communities, as long as such incentives are racially neutral and equitably available. She further suggests incentive programs for blacks to move into white neighborhoods as well as for whites to move into integrated neighborhoods, as such an effort would decrease the number of segregated communities nationally. While the particulars of such programs are likely debatable, the combination of affirmative marketing at the national level coupled with federal incentive programs is widely thought to nurture and uplift integrated communities. Again, this is all the more likely to be successful when paired with a frank discussion about racial inequality, both its roots and its modern manifestations, at the national level.

At the federal level, things like the Community Development Block Grant (CDBG) program, which is designed to provide housing and create jobs in low- and moderate-income communities, are key. Economically and racially diverse neighborhoods like the ones in this study would certainly benefit from such programs, as they would elevate the economic base for the populations most vulnerable to development and gentrification efforts. Obama's commitment to CDBG grants is certainly a step in the right direction, for they would provide a critical legitimacy and commitment to maintaining the diversity of the neighborhoods by targeting the needs of its most vulnerable residents. Obama's platform has also included plans to increase access to capital for underserved businesses, specifically minority-owned businesses. Plans such as these will help to ensure the maintenance of racial diversity in these communities by pairing with community members' desires to see a diverse business pool as well as a stable economic base. This backing would also help to offset the impact of development and gentrification efforts by making underserved and minority-owned businesses competitive in the real estate and consumer markets.

Finally, Obama's urban platform contains the promise of efforts to support teachers in urban schools, expand early childhood education, and reduce the high school dropout rate. Residents in this book demonstrated significant concern about the quality of public schools, with varying degrees of appreciation for the economic and structural forces that shape them. Elevating the public schools in diverse communities would not only continue to make them attractive places to live for whites who desire racial diversity, but more importantly, provide a key resource for low-income and minority populations who disproportionately attend them. While the school-focused community organizations were defunct at the time I conducted this research, the mechanism and history of community concern is present, and especially with the help of federal dollars and initiatives, provide one ready mechanism for sustaining racial diversity and quality of life for all residents. Juliet Saltman (1990) has argued that money and programming aimed toward minority populations in integrated communities can sustain diversity even when there is an undesired racial gap in leadership and few white parents sending their children into the public schools.

Unfortunately, these initiatives are not yet fully implemented, nor are they alone enough. While the above are promising leads, the bulk of Obama's federal urban policy is geared toward development. Unless carefully mediated, this could easily lead to gentrification and a loss of the racial diversity that has defined these communities for decades. Further, to date, the only action in this arena are select funds allocated through the American Recovery and Reinvestment Act. While much of this puts needed monies toward some of the efforts named above, the broader principles of the White House Office of Urban Affairs emphasizes growth and competition through green and high wage jobs. While inclusiveness and equity are stated as vital toward these efforts, without a break in the free market principles that have so often perpetuated segregation and gentrification to the benefit of whites and homeowners, or a stated commitment to economic and racial diversity, the results are likely to sustain the status quo. As Grigsby has suggested, "There is no such thing as a race-neutral policy" (1994, 240). Policies like the ones forged in these communities and at the federal level are fundamentally ambivalent, and unless made more strategic, are likely to reproduce tensions and undermine the community's stability.

While a boost to the local economy is sorely needed in many urban communities, this has too often coupled with a rise in property values that is untenable for affordable housing, which is key to the preservation of a diverse community like the ones in this book. Further, local pro-Obama residents like the ones in this book indicate a strong preference for market strength over affordable housing in these communities, and demonstrate their own ambivalence on matters related to diversity. Like Obama's urban policies, they demonstrate a broad appreciation for diversity, inclusiveness, and equity, and a desire to see safety and schooling concerns addressed. Yet without an overt, funded, and institutionally strong commitment to maintaining this diversity in the face of economic development and competition, the benefits are likely to continue to aggregate to the white homeowners whose real estate investments will increase, while potentially marginalizing or displacing low-income and racial minority populations. This is why national and federal recommendations are likely to fail without the accompanying local efforts and support.

Local Level Recommendations

It could be argued that the local efforts to sustain and support diversity in these communities are more important than those at the federal level. Along with national support, the affirmation of these communities at the local level is vital to their continued success. In particular, it has been widely recognized that an intentional commitment to the continued diversity in these communities is vital to local efforts, regardless of whether the communities began as diverse by direction or diverse by circumstance. Maly notes that the absence of indicators of rapid re-segregation "does not mean that diverse-by-circumstance communities' local efforts are not necessary to maintain the integration . . . conscious efforts . . . are required if integration is to be maintained over the long haul" (2006, 47)

The primacy of strategic planning has long been demonstrated for racially integrated communities and their efforts. Sol Tax, in documenting the efforts of Chicago's Hyde Park to become integrated rather than re-segregated in the 1950s, noted: "nothing at all could have been done if racial integration had not been an explicit and integral part of the plan . . . nothing would have happened without deliberate social action" (1959, 22). Juliet Saltman in a similar piece said, "Eternal vigilance is necessary to counteract the massive institutional forces that hasten neighborhood instability and re-segregation" (1990, 547). Finally, Nyden et al have noted that even in diverse-by-circumstance communities, "community-based initiatives also influence the diversity and stability of neighborhoods" (1998, 12). These are primarily created through coalitions, as the diverse pool of community groups work together toward common goals, which collectively sustain the diversity in these communities.

Currently, while the identities of Rogers Park, Edgewater, and Uptown are closely tied to their diversity, and while the diversity of these communities are proudly noted among its umbrella community organizations such as the Uptown Chicago Commission and the Edgewater Community Council, there lacks an explicit commitment to maintaining this diversity in these communities' initiatives. Making the choice as a community to add this commitment to both the spectrum of community initiatives as well as to their committee structures would be one simple step toward ensuring that the racial diversity in these communities is maintained.

Discussing the integration efforts of fifteen communities throughout the United States, Saltman outlines three trajectories community efforts toward sustained integration have taken: failed, conditional, and successful. She demonstrates that communities which have experienced conditional success exhibit the following qualities: vigorous racism alongside vigorous civil rights; a stated goal of integration; committees devoted to block level issues, schools, housing, and business development; a disbanded school committee; nonintegrated schools; a varied amount of both housing stock and housing maintenance, where units range from public housing to mansions; and inconsistent funding. This is almost verbatim a description of Rogers Park, Edgewater, and Uptown at the time I conducted this research in 2007–2009.

While I encountered very little outright racism in these communities, there does exist a vibrant online community which is quite brazen about its monitoring of poor people of color in these communities. While small in number, members of this community are widely read and have been known to mobilize during election years and when other key issues are at stake. Thankfully, their presence is offset by those I interviewed in this study who care very much about the diversity in these communities and showed a commitment to equality and civil rights. This balance, itself, is an affirmation of one of Saltman's criteria for conditional success. On the other hand, an explicit policy of integration remains lacking in these communities. While an appreciation and acknowledgement is present in most community and political statements in these communities, it is not a pledge, promise, or goal. Here the communities demonstrate one area for improvement should they collectively decide that their diversity is worthy of being maintained.

Further, all three communities contain segregated schools. Recent reports from interviewees indicate that the schooling committees have become defunct in recent years, and while the public schools house an incredibly diverse nonwhite population, there are very few white students in attendance. None of the white residents in this study sent their children to the local public schools. Perhaps it is difficult for one middle class white parent to make the choice to send their children into the public schools in these communities, but what if all of the parents made a pact to do so, and invested their tax dollars, private donations, and energies to the schools to make them better places and ensure the resources for a quality education? What if the community organizations were to throw their marketing power and monies into the schools, and in turn tout these diverse, successful schools as a vital asset to the community? If CAPS has been such a strong (albeit contested) model for community policing, then why not engage community education? Doing everything imaginable to support and sustain the community's schools may be the most equitable work sustaining diversity that these community groups could begin.

Actively engaging antidiscrimination laws are also a significant piece of the ongoing project of sustaining diverse communities. The Lakeside CDC report published in 2006 highlighted the reality that both discrimination and free market principles were working together to undermine the diversity in Rogers Park, primarily through a loss of rental housing. While studying these realities is important, and strengthening the laws and policies around equal housing are vital, Nyden et al note that "The laws alone cannot create diversity—the hands of local activists are required" (1998, 266). I was encouraged to learn, after my study was complete and I had moved away for work, that there had been active efforts to support residents being foreclosed on in these communities.

Finally, not only disseminating positive media and marketing around diverse communities, but also responding responsibly to negative stories, blogs, and perceptions of these communities is vital. Those who are already living and working in diverse communities can play a crucial role in paving the way for others—when it is no longer so odd to make one's home and forge one's community in places like these, other communities are sure to follow. While the presence of color-blind ideologies and limited diversity discourses do not indicate that these communities are by any means perfect, the presence of an engaged, active, caring community who talks about and respects its racial diversity provides, if not a perfect model for our nation's future, then at least a humble, fragile, but promising beginning.

THE PATH AHEAD

The early figures from the 2010 Census indicate that people of color are leaving the city, and more whites are moving in. While the three communities that I studied for this book seem to be maintaining their racial diversity, like all communities, theirs will likely continue to be one of change and contested politics. That said, if the pro-diversity, caring, and committed residents in this book, and any who follow in their footsteps, can come together and work on diversity as a key community initiative, I believe that they can maintain the diversity that they cherish. They are taking the first fragile steps onto a path that an increasing number of communities around the nation may walk as our racial and ethnic diversity grows. While at times their footing has been unsteady, I believe that they, and we as a nation, can learn to move past the color-blind ideologies that render us speechless, and begin real conversations about race and democracy in our communities and in our nation.

BIBLIOGRAPHY

Andersen, Margaret L. 1999. "Diversity without Oppression: Race, Ethnicity, Identity, and Power. Pp. 5–20 in *Critical Ethnicity: Countering the Waves of Identity Politics*. Totowa, NJ: Rowman & Littlefield Publishers.

Anderson, Elijah. 2000. *Code of the Street: Decency, Violence, and the Moral Life of the Inner City*. New York: W. W. Norton & Co.

Anderson, Elijah. 2011. *The Cosmopolitan Canopy: Race and Civility in Everyday Life*. New York: W. W. Norton & Co.

Barlow, Andrew L. 2003. *Between Fear and Hope: Globalization and Race in the United States*. New York: Rowman & Littlefield Publishers.

Beeman, Angie K. 2007. "Emotional Segregation: A Content Analysis of Institutional Racism in US Films: 1980–2001," *Ethnic and Racial Studies* 30(5): 687–712.

Bell, Joyce M. and Douglas Hartmann. 2007. "Diversity in Everyday Discourse: The Cultural Ambiguities and Consequences of 'Happy Talk.'" *American Sociological Review* 72: 895-914,

Bennett, Larry. 1993. "Rethinking Neighborhoods, Neighborhood Research, and Neighborhood Policy: Lessons from Uptown." *Journal of Urban Affairs* 15(3): 245–257.

Blee, Kathleen. 1991. *Woman of the Klan: Racism and Gender in the 1920s*. Berkeley: University of California Press.

Bonilla-Silva, Eduardo and Tyrone Forman. 2000. "I'm Not a Racist but . . .': Mapping White College Students' Racial Ideology in the USA." *Discourse & Society* 11(1): 49–85.

Bonilla-Silva, Eduardo. 2001. *White Supremacy & Racism in the Post-Civil Rights Era*. Boulder: Lynne Rienner Publishers.

Bonilla-Silva, Eduardo. 2003. *Racism without Racists: Color-Blind Racism and the Persistence of Racial Inequality in the United States*. Rowman & Littlefield Publishers.

Bonilla-Silva, Eduardo, Amanda Lewis, and David G. Embrick. 2004. "'I Did Not Get That Job Because of a Black Man . . .': The Story Lines and Testimonies of Color-Blind Racism." *Sociological Forum* 1984): 555–581.

Bonilla-Silva, Eduardo and David Embrick. 2007. "'Every Place Has a Ghetto . . .': The Significance of Whites' Social and Residential Segregation." *Symbolic Interaction* 30(3): 323–345.

Charles, Camille Zubrinsky. 2000. "Neighborhood Racial-Composition Preferences: Evidence from a Multiethnic Metropolis." *Social Problems* 47(3): 379–407.

Charles, Camille Zubrinsky. 2003. "The Dynamics of Racial Residential Segregation." *Annual Review of Sociology* 29: 167–207.

Charles, Camille Zubrinsky. 2006. *Won't You Be My Neighbor: Race, Class, and Residence in Los Angeles*. New York: Russell Sage Foundation.

Chicago Fact Finder. 2009. *Chicago Fact Finder*. Institute for Latino Studies at Notre Dame University. (http://www.nd.edu/~chifacts/index.html)

Chicago Police Department. 2007. "Overall Crime in Chicago Continues to Decrease in Every Major Category for 2006." Checkerboard Chat: Official Blog of the Chicago Police Department. (http://cpdweblog.typepad.com/chicago_police_department/crime_statistics/index.html)

Chicago Police Department. 2009. *CLEARMAP: Crime Summary Reports*. Generated for Homocide 1st & 2nd Degree; Aggrivated Assault; Violent Crime; and Index Crime on February 26, 2009. (http://gis.chicagopolice.org/)

Compton-Lilly, C. (2003). *Reading Families: The Literate Lives of Urban Children*. New York: Teachers College Press.

Croll, Paul. 2007. "Modeling Determinants of White Racial Identity: Results from a New National Survey." *Social Forces* 86(2): 613–642.

CURL. 2006. "Segregation in Chicago 2006: Executive Summary." Center for Urban Research and Learning at Loyola University Chicago. (http://www.cfm40.org)

de Beauvoir, Simone. 1989 [1953]. *The Second Sex*. New York: Vintage Books.

Devault, Marjorie L. 1990. "Talking and Listening from Women's Standpoint: Feminist Strategies for Interviewing and Analysis." *Social Problems* 37(1): 96–116.

Dirks, Danielle and Stephen K. Rice. "Dining While Black: Racial Rituals and the Black American Restaurant Experience." *Race and Ethnicity: Across Time, Space, and Discipline*. Leiden, Netherlands: Brill.

Ebert, Kimberly L. 2001. "The Threat of Gentrification: The Response to Displacement and the Loss of Affordable Housing in an Economically, Racially, and Ethnically Diverse Chicago Community." M.A. Thesis, Department of Sociology, Loyola University Chicago, Chicago.

Edgewater Community Council. 1986. *Preserving the Housing of Central Edgewater: A Plan for Action*. A Report Prepared for the City of Chicago Department of Housing.

Edgewater Community Council (ECC). 2009. "About Us." Edgewater Community Council website. (http://edgewatercommunitycouncil.org/home/Home/aboutus)

Edgewater Historical Society. 1991. "Edgewater Beach." *1991 Fall Tour of Homes*.

Eichstedt, Jennifer L. 2001. "Problematic White Identities and a Search for Racial Justice." *Sociological Forum* 6(3): 445–470.

Ellen, Ingrid Gould. 2000. *Sharing America's Neighborhoods: The Prospects for Stable Racial Integration*. Cambridge: Harvard University Press.

Ellis, Mark and Richard Wright. 2004. "Work Together, Live Apart?: Geographies of Racial and Ethnic Segregation at Home and Work." *Annals of the Association of American Geographers* 94(3): 620–637.

Emerson, Michael O., Rachel Tolbert Kimbro, and George Yancey. 2002. "Contact Theory Extended: The Effects of Prior Racial Contact on Current Social Ties." *Social Science Quarterly* 83(3): 745–761.

Farley, Reynolds and William H. Frey. 1994. "Changes in the Segregation of Whites from Blacks During the 1980s: Small Steps Toward a More Integrated Society." *American Sociological Review* 59(1): 23–45.

Fischer, Lauren and Joseph P. Schwieterman. 2008. *A Kaleidoscope of Culture: Measuring the Diversity of Chicago's Neighborhoods*. DePaul University: School of Public Service Policy Study.

Feagin, Joe R. 2006. *Systemic Racism: A Theory of Oppression*. New York: Routledge.

Feagin, Joe R. 2010. *The White Racial Frame: Centuries of Racial Framing and Counter-Framing*. New York: Routledge.

Forman, Tyrone. 2004. "Color-Blind Racism and Racial Indifference: The Role of Apathy in Facilitating Enduring Inequalities." Pp. 43–66 in *The Changing Terrain of Race and Ethnicity*. New York: Russell Sage Foundation.

Foster, John D. 2009. "Defending Whiteness Indirectly: A Synthetic Approach to Race Discourse Analysis." *Discourse & Society* 20(6): 685–703.

Frankenburg, Ruth. 1999. *White Women, Race Matters: The Social Construction of Whiteness*. Minneapolis: University of Minnesota Press.

Gallagher, Charles. 1995. "White Reconstruction in the University." *Socialist Review* 94 (1&2): 165–187.

Gallagher, Charles. 2000. "White Like Me?: Methods, Meaning, and Manipulation in the Field of White Studies." Pp. 67–92 in *Race-ing Research, Researching Race: Methodological and Ethical Dilemmas in Field Research*. New York: New York University Press.

Gitlin, Todd and Nanci Hollander. 1970. *Uptown: Poor Whites in Chicago*. New York: Harper and Row.

Grigsby, J. Eugene III. 1994. "In Planning There Is No Such Thing as a 'Race Neutral' Policy." *Journal of the American Planning Association* 60(2): 240–241.

Hartmann, Doug, Joseph Gertis, and Paul Croll. 2009. "An Empirical Assessment of Whiteness Theory: Hidden from How Many?" *Social Problems* 56 (3): 403–424.

Hill, Jane H. 2008. *The Everyday Language of White Racism*. West Sussex, UK: Wiley-Blackwell.

Hill Collins, Patricia. 2000. *Black Feminist Thought: Knowledge, Consciousness, and the Politics of Empowerment*. New York: Routledge.

Holder, Eric. 2009. "Remarks as Prepared for Delivery by Attorney Eric Holder at the Department of Justice African American History Month Program." Wednesday, February 18, 2009. (http://www.usdoj.gov/ag/speeches/2009/ag-speech-090218.html)

Holthouse, David. 2009. "The Year in Hate: Number of Hate Groups Tops 900." Southern Poverty Law Center *Intelligence Report*, Spring 2009. (http://www.splcenter.org/intel/intelreport/article.jsp?aid=1027)

Hughey, Matthew W. 2010. "A Paradox of Participation: Nonwhites in White Sororities and Fraternities." *Social Problems* 57(4): 653–679.

Iversen, Roberta Rehner and Naomi B. Farber. 1996. "Transmission of Family Values, Work, and Welfare among Poor Urban Black Women." *Work and Occupations*, 23(4): 437–460.

Johnson, Heather Beth and Thomas M. Shapiro. 2003. "Good Neighborhoods, Good Schools: Race and the 'Good Choices' of White Families." Pp. 173–187 in Eduardo Bonilla-Silva and Woody Doane, eds., *White Out: The Continuing Significance of Racism*. New York: Routledge.

Klinenberg, Eric. 2002. *Heat Wave: A Social Autopsy of Disaster in Chicago*. Chicago: University of Chicago Press.

Krysan, Maria. 2002. "Whites Who Say They'd Flee: Who Are They, and Why Would They Leave?" *Demography* 39(4): 675–696.

Krysan, Maria and Reynolds Farley. 2002. "The Residential Preferences of Blacks: Do They Explain Persistent Segregation?" *Social Forces* 80: 937–980.

Lakeside CDC. 2006. *The Community Housing Audit: Housing Redevelopment in One Chicago Neighborhood*. Lakeside Community Development Corporation. (http://www.lakesidecdc.org)

Lareau, A., & Horvat, E. (1999). Moments of Social Inclusion and Exclusion: Race, Class, and Cultural Capital in Family-school Relationships. *Sociology of Education* 72 37–53.

Lewis, Amanda. 2003. *Race in the Schoolyard: Negotiating the Color Line in Classrooms and Communities*. New Brunswick: Rutgers University Press.

Lewis, Amanda. 2004. "'What Group?': Studying Whites and Whiteness in the Era of 'Color-Blindness.'" *Sociological Theory* 22(4): 623–646.

Logan, John R., Richard D. Alba, and Wenquan Zhang. 2002. "Immigrant Enclves and Ethnic Communities in New York and Los Angeles." *American Sociological Review* 67(2): 299–322.

Lowndes, Vivian. 2000. "Women and Social Capital." *British Journal of Political Science* 30(3): 533–537.

Maly, Michael T. 2006. *Beyond Segregation: Multiracial and Multiethnic Neighborhoods in the United States*. Philadelphia: Temple University Press.

Maly, Michael T. 2005. *Beyond Segregation: Multiracial and Multiethnic-Neighborhoods in the United States*. Philadelphia: Temple University Press.

Maly, Michael T. and Michael Leachman. 1998. "Chapter 7: Rogers Park, Edgewater, Uptown, and Chicago Lawn, Chicago." *Cityscape: A Journal of Policy Development and Research* 4(2): 131–160.

Marciniak, Ed. 1981. *Reversing Urban Decline: The Winthrop-Kenmore Corridor in the Edgewater and Uptown Communities of Chicago*. Washington, DC: National Center for Urban Ethnic Affairs.

Martinez-Cosio, Maria L. 2007. "Coloring Housing Changes: Reintroducing Race into Gentrification" Paper presented at the annual meeting of the American Sociological Association. New York. (http://www.allacademic.com/meta/p181847_index.html)

Massey, Douglas S. and Nancy A. Denton. 1993. *American Apartheid: Segregation and the Making of the Underclass*. Cambridge: Harvard University Press.

McIntosh, Peggy. 2005. "White Privilege: Unpacking the Invisible Knapsack." Pp. 109–113 in *White Privilege: Essential Readings on the Other Side of Racism*. New York: Worth Publishers.

Mitchell, Robert Edward. 1971. "Some Social Implications of High Density Housing." *American Sociological Review* 36: 18–29.

Moody, James. "Race, School Integration, and Friendship Segregation in America." *American Journal of Sociology* 107(3): 679–716.

Mooney-Melvin, Patricia. 1993. *Reading Your Neighborhood: A Brief History of East Rogers Park*. Chicago: Loyola University.

Mooney-Melvin, Patricia. 2008. "Rogers Park." *The Encyclopedia of Chicago*, edited by the Chicago History Museum. (http://www.encyclopedia.chicago-history.org/pages/1086.html)

Moynihan, Daniel Patrick and Nathan Glazer. 1970. *Beyond the Melting Pot*. 2nd ed. Cambridge: MIT Press.

Myers, Kristin. 2005. *Racetalk: Racism Hiding in Plain Sight*. Boulder, CO: Rowman & Littlefield Publishers.

Niemonen, Jack. 2010. "Public Sociology or Partisan Sociology: The Curious Case of Whiteness Studies." *American Sociologist* 41(1): 48–82.

Nyden, Philip, Emily Edlynn, and Julie Davis. 2006. "The Differential Impact of Gentrification on Communities in Chicago. Loyola Center for Urban Research and Learning, for the City of Chicago Council on Human Relations." January 2006. (http://www.luc.edu/curl/publications.shtml)

Nyden, Philip, John Lukehart, Michael T. Maly, and William Peterman. 1998. "Neighborhood Racial and Ethnic Diversity in U.S. Cities." *Cityscape: A Journal of Policy Development and Research* 4(2): 1–17.

O'Brien, Eileen. 2008. *The Racial Middle: Latinos and Asian Americans Living Beyond the Racial Divide*. New York: New York University Press.

Oliver, J. Eric. 2000. "City Size and Civic Involvement in Metropolitan America." *American Political Science Review* 94(2): 361–373.

Omi, Michael and Howard Winant. 1994. *Racial Formation in the United States From the 1960s to the 1990s, 2nd ed.*. New York: Routledge.

Organization of the Northeast (ONE). 2009. Organization of the Northeast website. (http://www.onechicago.org)

Outside.In. 2008. *Inside America's Top 10 Bloggiest Neighborhoods*. (http://outside.in/public/bloggiest_neighborhoods)

Pattillo-McCoy, Mary. 2001. Review of "Sharing America's Neighborhoods: The Prospects for Stable Racial Integration by Ingrid Gould Ellen." *American Journal of Sociology* 106(6): 1816–1818.

Perry, Pamela. 2001. "White Means Never Having to Say You're Ethnic: White Youth and the Construction of 'Cultureless' Identities." *Journal of Contemporary Ethnography* 30(1): 56–91.

Picca, Leslie Houts and Joe R. Feagin. 2007. *Two-Faced Racism: Whites in the Backstage and Frontstage*. New York: Routledge.

Popkin, Susan J, Victoria E. Gwiasda, Lynn M. Olson, Dennis P. Rosenbaum, and Larry Buron. 2000. *Hidden War: Crime and the Tragedy of Public Housing in Chicago*. New Jersey: Rutgers University Press.

Putnam, Robert. 2000. *Bowling Alone: The Collapse and Revival of American Community*. New York: Simon & Schuster.

Rodriquez, Jason. 2006. "Color-Blind Ideology and the Cultural Appropriation of Hip-Hop." *Journal of Contemporary Ethnography* 35(6): 645–668.

Roediger, David R. 2005. *Working Toward Whiteness: How America's Immigrant's Became White. The Strange Journey from Ellis Island to the Suburbs*. New York: Basic Books.

Saltman, Juliet. 1990. "Neighborhood Stabilization: A Fragile Movement." *Sociological Quarterly* 31(4): 531–549.

Saxe, L., Kadushin, C., Tighe, E., Rindskopf, D., and Beveridge, A. (2001). *National Evaluation of the Fighting Back Program: General Population Surveys, 1995–1999*. New York: City University of New York Graduate Center.

Schaefer, Richard. 1996. "Presidential Address-Education and Prejudice: Unraveling the Relationship." *Sociological Quarterly* 37(1): 1–16.

Schweitzerman, Joseph P. and Dana M. Caspall. 2006. *The Politics of Place: A History of Zoning in Chicago*. Chicago: Lake Claremont Press.

Seligman, Amanda. 2008a. "Edgewater." *The Encyclopedia of Chicago*, edited by the Chicago History Museum. (http://www.encyclopedia.chicagohistory.org/pages/413.html)

Seligman, Amanda. 2008b. "Uptown." *The Encyclopedia of Chicago*, edited by the Chicago History Museum. (http://www.encyclopedia.chicagohistory.org/pages/1293.html)

Shaw, Samuel C. and Sullivan, Daniel M. 2007. "Gentrification and Racial Boundaries." Paper presented at the annual meeting of the American Sociological Association, Montreal Convention Center, Montreal, Quebec, Canada. (http://www.allacademic.com/meta/p104876_index.html)

Smith, Dorothy. 1990. *The Conceptual Practices of Power: A Feminist Sociology of Knowledge*. Boston: Northeastern University Press.

Smith, Mary Ann. 2009. "Community Input Key to Decision Making." Website for Alderman Mary Ann Smith. (http://www.masmith48.org/economicdevelopment.html#article2)

Smith, Neil. 1979. "Toward a Theory of Gentrification." *Journal of the American Planning Association* 45(4): 538–548.

Smith, Neil. 1998. "Building the Frontier Myth." Pp. 12–18 in *Introduction to The New Urban Frontier*. New York: Routledge.

Steyn, Melissa and Don Foster. 2008. "Repertoires for talking white: Resistant whiteness in post-apartheid South Africa" *Ethnic and Racial Studies* 31(1): 25–51.

Tatum, Beverly. 2003. *"Why Are All the Black Kids Sitting Together in the Cafeteria?" And Other Conversations About Race*. New York: Basic Books.

Tax, Sol. 1959. "Residential Integration: The Case of Hyde Park in Chicago." *Human Organization* 18(1): 22–27.

Taylor, Marylee C. 1998. "How White Attitudes Vary with the Racial Composition of Local Populations: Numbers Count." *American Sociological Review* 63: 512–535.

Thompson, Becky. 2010. "Subverting Racism from Within: Linking White Identity to Activism." pp. 213–232 in *Privilege: A Reader*, 2nd ed. Edited by Michael S. Kimmel and Abby L. Ferber. Bounder, CO: Westview Press.

Twine, France Winddance and Charles Gallagher. 2008. "The Future of Whiteness: A Map of the 'Third Wave.'" *Ethnic and Racial Studies* 31(1): 4–24.

Twine, France Winddance and Amy C. Steinbugler. 2006. "The Gap between Whites and Whiteness: Interracial Intimacy and Racial Literacy." *DuBois Review* 3(2): 341–363.

Uptown Chicago Commission (UCC). 2009. "About Us." Uptown Chicago Commission website. (http://www.uptownchicagocommission.org/about. htm)

Van den Berg, Harry. 2003. "Contradictions in Interview Discourse." Pp. 119–137 in *Analyzing Race Talk: Multidisciplinary Approaches to the Interview*. Edited by Harry van den Berg, Margaret Wetherell, and Hanneke Houtkoop-Steenstra. Cambridge, MA: Cambridge University Press.

Wegener, E. 1979. "Community Crime Prevention–A Neighborhood Action Guide." *Civic Action Institute*. U.S. Department of Housing and Urban Development.

West, Candace and Don Zimmerman. 1987. "Doing Gender." *Gender and Society* 1(2): 125–151.

Wilson, William Julius. 1997. *When Work Disappears*. New York: Random House.

Wilson, William Julius and Richard P. Taub. 2006. *There Goes the Neighborhood: Racial, Ethnic, and Class Tensions in Four Chicago Neighborhoods and Their Meaning for America*. New York: Knopf.

Yancey, George. 1999. "An Examination of the Effects of Residential and Church Integration on Racial Attitudes of Whites." *Sociological Perspectives* 42(2): 279–304.

Zamudio, Margaret and Francisco Rios. 2006. "From Traditional to Liberal Racism: Living Racism in the Everyday." *Sociological Perspectives* 49(4): 237–269.

Zajicek, Anna M. 2002. "Race Discourses and Antiracist Practices in a Local Women's Movement." *Gender and Society* 16(2): 155–174.

INDEX

CPSIA information can be obtained at www.ICGtesting.com
Printed in the USA
BVOW010449140612

292577BV00002B/1/P